The Holy Spirit in the Wesleyan Heritage

Mack B. Stokes

Graded Press / Abingdon Press
Nashville, Tennessee

The Holy Spirit in the Wesleyan Heritage

Trade Edition Distributed by Abingdon Press.

Library of Congress Cataloging in Publication Data

STOKES, MACK B.
The Holy Spirit in the Wesleyan heritage.
1. Holy Spirit—History of doctrines. 2. Holy Spirit—
Biblical teaching. 3. Wesley, John, 1703–1791.
I. Title.
BT119.S76   1985   231′.044   85-6146
(pbk. : alk. paper)

ISBN 0-687-17310-8

An official resource of The United Methodist Church prepared by
the General Board of Discipleship through the Curriculum
Resources Committee and published by Graded Press, P. O. Box
801, Nashville, Tennessee 37202. Printed in the United States of
America.

H. Claude Young, Jr.
Editor, Church School Publications

Nellie M. Moser
Editor, Youth and Adult Resources and Editor of
THE HOLY SPIRIT IN THE WESLEYAN HERITAGE

Marcia Catlin Ryan
Assistant Editor

Gordon Gullette
Design Director

Cover design by
Gordon Gullette

Contents

Introduction

The Distinctively Christian Idea of God

Christians have always believed in one God. They have affirmed monotheism (belief in one God) in contrast to all forms of polytheism (belief in many gods). At the same time, Christians have declared on the basis of Scripture that this one God is to be understood as Father, Son, and Holy Spirit. Therefore God is three-in-one. This is the doctrine of the Trinity.

Many efforts have been made to explain this doctrine. Some thinkers have used the analogy of something physical, such as water, to explain it. Water may be in the form of liquid, steam, or ice, but its chemical formula is still H_2O. Others, including Augustine, have tried to explain the Trinity in terms of our personal characteristics. A person may be thought of as having three aspects such as intellect, feeling, and will. These are three-in-one. But after all efforts to explain have been exhausted, the doctrine of the Trinity remains a mystery. God is revealed as Father, Son, and Holy Spirit, but *how* God can be three-in-one has not been revealed.

John Wesley said:

I believe . . . that God is Three and One. But the *manner how* I do not comprehend; and I do not believe it. Now in this, in the *manner*, lies the mystery; and so it may; I have no concern with it: It is no object of my faith: I believe just so much as God has revealed, and no more. But this, the *manner*, he has not revealed; therefore I believe nothing about it. But would it not be absurd in me to deny the fact, because I do not understand the manner? That is, to reject *what God has revealed*, because I do not comprehend *what he has not revealed*. [From *The Works of John Wesley*, Volume VI (Zondervan Publishing House, 1959), page 204]

We do not turn away from any doctrine or belief merely because it involves mystery. Indeed, we are surrounded by mystery in everyday life. Life itself is a mystery, but we live it. *How* the body and soul can be interacting with each other, we do not know. But *that* they are, we do know. Belief in the Trinity is a matter of faith based on the biblical revelation.

Practically speaking, and this was Wesley's primary concern, the doctrine of the Trinity means that God has revealed himself in three ways that bear directly on our lives as human beings.

As the Father, God is our Creator, Sustainer, and Provider. We are ever-dependent on God who gives to all people "life and breath and everything" (Acts 17:25).

As the Son, God is the Redeemer who pardons our sins and brings us into a dynamic and right relationship with God.

As the Holy Spirit, God comes near to us, draws us to Jesus Christ, and enables us to receive Jesus into our hearts as Savior and Lord. The Holy Spirit comforts us, sustains us in every good work, and binds us into the living fellowship of believers.

Father, Son, and Holy Spirit are mysteriously interrelated in their unity of being and purpose in all these activities. But God *reveals himself* in these different dynamic activities in relation to us.

Therefore, the Trinity means that God relates to us in three *specifiable ways*. Such relating is not possible when we try to worship a deity of an unspecified nature that has not been revealed at this point. The significance of Wesley's stress on the practical importance of the doctrine of the Trinity lies in his belief that what God has revealed about himself is of utmost importance. "It enters into the very heart of Christianity: It lies at the root of all vital religion" (*Works*, Volume VI, page 205).

The Holy Spirit in the Trinity

The work of the Holy Spirit should be understood within the total context of the Trinity. Why? Because otherwise much that is important in the biblical revelation is missed. Some Christians concentrate so much on the Holy Spirit that they lose sight of the full divine revelation. We need to understand that God is the Creator and Sustainer of the universe. We need to know that God is the Redeemer of the whole world of human beings. The mission of the Holy Spirit is directly related to the purpose of God in creation and redemption.

The Bible teaches that God created human beings for a purpose. God has a plan for persons to enjoy fellowship with him while actively working in God's kingdom. God acted in Jesus Christ to save the lost and re-create them for fellowship and for service in God's kingdom. Why the Holy Spirit? The Holy Spirit acts to carry forward that same purpose of realizing all the precious values God wants for us in the Kingdom. In all this activity the key word is *purpose*.

God never does anything by accident or blind chance. We were created and redeemed for a purpose. God moves into our souls through the Holy Spirit for a purpose. And that holy purpose is one.

God's revealed *purpose* for every human being is this: to realize moral and spiritual values in community under Jesus Christ as Savior and Lord and by the presence and power of the Holy Spirit. In other words, God's purpose is to realize the Kingdom through the power of the Holy Spirit working in us. By nature, the Holy Spirit is dynamic and purposeful, acting to draw us to the Savior and to empower us for mission. All of the Holy Spirit's gifts and manifestations, whether universal or special, are "for the common good" (1 Corinthians 12:7). Within the churches they are for building up the "body of Christ" (12:27). Outside the churches they are for blessing people at home and at work and for making disciples of people everywhere.

The Holy Spirit is God manifesting himself in important and special ways on our behalf. As Wesley said:

> By faith I know that the Holy Spirit is the giver of all spiritual life; of righteousness, peace, joy in the Holy Ghost; of holiness and happiness, by the restoration of that image of God wherein we are created. (*Works*, Volume VII, page 233)

CHAPTER 1

The Spirit in the Old Testament

The main word for "spirit" in the Old Testament is *rūach*. Literally, it means "wind" or "breath." Sometimes it means "life." When used in reference to God, the word suggests the awesome power and energy of God in action in this world. Sometimes this energy of the Spirit of God is specific; sometimes universal or general. But it is always according to God's own choosing. In the highest expression, the Spirit is moral and compassionate (Isaiah 61:1-4; Zechariah 4:1-10).

In the most intimately personal expression, the Spirit of God is said to know the human soul and to be ever-present with it (Psalm 139). It is important to remember that God's involvement with people is expressed also without the use of the word *rūach*. We read of the finger of God, the hand, the arm, the name, the glory, the Word, the messengers of God. The God of the Old Testament is, then, the Spirit who lives and acts in the here and now.

Let us turn now to consider the specific ways in which the Spirit of God has acted and continues to act.

The Spirit in Creation and Providence

God has been revealed as dynamically at work throughout the universe. The first account of Creation reads: "and the Spirit of God was moving over the face of the waters" (Genesis 1:2).

According to the Old Testament God is dynamic, active, and radically involved in the whole realm of nature.

Thus the biblical writers are opposed to the view that God is wholly above and beyond the created world. Some theologians from ancient times to the present have said that God is too great and too perfect to be involved in this present universe. But the Bible does not teach this.

The biblical view also stands in contrast to Deism (the idea that God created the universe and left it to run by itself). Deism correctly affirms the Creator, but it misses the fact that God created for a purpose—or a network of purposes—yet to be realized. So God's *continuing creative energies* are necessary. The biblical writers recognized this fact.

We read that God is the one "who stretches out the heavens like a curtain" (Isaiah 40:22). God presides as "the king of all the earth" (Psalm 47:7). God's energy touches the "highest heavens" (Psalm 148:4) and renews the face of the earth (Psalm 104:30). In God's hands are the deep places of land and sea (Psalm 95:4-5). The winds are God's messengers, fire and flame God's ministers (Psalm 104:3-4). God gives the sun for a light by day and stars for a light by night (Jeremiah 31:35). God sends the rains and provides the basis for agriculture (Leviticus 26:4; Deuteronomy 11:14; 28:12; Job 5:10; Psalm 65:9-10; 68:9; 104:10-13; 147:8; Jeremiah 14:22). And Jesus continued this heritage from the Old Testament (Matthew 5:45).

God, then, created and creates. God is radically involved in the whole realm of nature and this involvement has a direct bearing on God's involvement with us.

At the same time, the biblical writers are never lured into Pantheism, the belief that God is everything that exists. Though intimately related to the universe, God is far more than the sum total of things. This truth is stated or implied throughout the Old Testament. It is stated with sublime inspiration in Job, Chapters 38–42. The New Testament tells us that God is "above all and through all and in all" (Ephesians 4:6; see also Acts 17:24-28; Romans 1:19-20;

11:36; 1 Corinthians 8:6). And these words were informed by the inspired authors of the Old Testament.

In summary so far, one of the most distinctive affirmations in the Old Testament is that God is always at work in and throughout the earth and the universe. It all belongs to God. For "the earth is the LORD's and the fulness thereof. . . ." (Psalm 24:1; see 1 Corinthians 10:26).

The Spirit at Work in the People of Israel

Against this background the inspired writers of the Old Testament take us into their main emphasis: the work of the Spirit of God in human beings. The teaching on God as the Lord of the Universe provides the atmosphere in which the Spirit's activity in human history can thrive. The same God who created the universe and all creatures has taken the initiative to realize his grand purpose in and through people. The Spirit of God created them. As we read in the Book of Job:

> The spirit of God has made me,
> and the breath of the Almighty gives me life. (33:4)

Think of it! The God of the universe—the Creator and Sustainer—is always taking the initiative in our behalf. This revealed theme of God's self-giving love begins in the Old Testament where we read of the Spirit of God at work among people.

The primary concern of the Spirit of God was to make people righteous. At times the Spirit moved suddenly and unexpectedly in the prophets and among the people. But the Spirit of God was not revealed as raw power, but as power with moral force.

> Woe to the rebellious children, says the LORD,
> who carry out a plan, but not mine;
> and who make a league, but not of my spirit,
> that they may add sin to sin.
> (Isaiah 30:1)

Further in the Book of Isaiah, a great prophet says:

> The Spirit of the Lord GOD is upon me,
>   because the LORD has anointed me
> to bring good tidings to the afflicted;
>   he has sent me to bind up the brokenhearted,
> to proclaim liberty to the captives. (61:1)

The prophet Micah expressed this same moral concern.

> But as for me, I am filled with power,
>   with the Spirit of the LORD,
>   and with justice and might,
> to declare to Jacob his transgression
>   and to Israel his sin. (3:8)

The psalmists, too, felt the Spirit of God moving them to reflect this passion for righteousness.

> Create in me a clean heart, O God,
>   and put a new and right spirit within me.
> Cast me not away from thy presence,
>   and take not thy holy Spirit from me.
>   (Psalm 51:10-11)

And again:

> Teach me to do thy will,
>   for thou art my God!
> Let thy good spirit lead me
>   on a level path!
>   (Psalm 143:10)

Zechariah brings this theme to a magnificent summary in the familiar words: "Not by might, nor by power, but by my Spirit, says the LORD of hosts" (4:6).

Along with the revelation of God's concern to bring righteousness into the hearts of the people of Israel came special manifestations of the Spirit. For example, the Spirit of God gave people special skills, including artistic ability. Of Bezalel we read: "I have filled him with the Spirit of God, with ability and intelligence, with knowledge and all craftsmanship, to devise artistic designs, to work in gold, silver, and bronze, in cutting stones for setting, and in carving wood, for work in every craft" (Exodus 31:3-5; see also 35:31-35).

Again, the Spirit gave leadership ability to selected individuals. The Spirit was in Moses and through him came upon the seventy elders who helped Moses "bear the burden of the people" (Numbers 11:17). Joshua was to succeed Moses because the Spirit was in him (27:18). The Spirit came upon Othniel to help him be a good judge in Israel (Judges 3:10). The Spirit of God was at work in Gideon (6:34) and in Jephthah (11:29). Even Samson's giant strength came from the Spirit of God (14:6).

When Saul was chosen to be the first king of Israel, Samuel said to him, "the Spirit of the LORD will come mightily upon you, and you shall prophecy . . . and be turned into another man" (1 Samuel 10:6; 11:6). Also, "the Spirit of the LORD came mightily upon David" who succeeded Saul (16:13; 23:1-2). In fact, the only genuine leaders in Israel were those under the influence of the Spirit.

The Spirit of God inspired the prophets. Consider the case of Ezekiel. The ecstatic experiences of this prophet were attributed to the Spirit. The Spirit commissioned Ezekiel to go to the people of Israel and tell them that they had sinned and had turned away from God (2:2-3). Ezekiel said, "And the Spirit of the LORD fell upon me. . . ." (11:5). Again and again Ezekiel tells of the Spirit lifting him up (3:12, 14; 8:3; 11:1, 24; 43:5). Under the influence of the Spirit, Ezekiel gave God's promise to the people. "A new heart I will give you, and a new spirit I will put within you. . . . And I will put my Spirit within you, and cause you to walk in my statutes and be careful to observe my ordinances" (36:26-27).

The Spirit of God was also in the *people* of Israel. The Lord made a covenant with the people, saying, "My spirit which is upon you, and my words which I have put in your mouth, shall not depart out of your mouth, or out of the mouth of your children, or out of the mouth of your children's children, says the LORD, from this time forth and for evermore" (Isaiah 59:21; see also Nehemiah 9:20; Haggai 2:5). This belief that the Spirit of God had chosen the people of Israel for a special mission in the world has been a prime factor in the thinking of Israel since the great event of the Exodus.

God promised to send a future leader of the people, in the line of David, who would be endowed with the Spirit.

> There shall come forth a shoot from the stump of Jesse,
> and a branch shall grow out of his roots.
> And the Spirit of the LORD shall rest upon him,
> the spirit of wisdom and understanding,
> the spirit of counsel and might,
> the spirit of knowledge and the fear of the LORD.
>
> (Isaiah 11:1-2)

This promise was for the whole people of Israel and for the whole world. In Isaiah 42:1, 4 we read:

> Behold my servant, whom I uphold,
> my chosen, in whom my soul delights;
> I have put my Spirit upon him,
> he will bring forth justice to the nations. . . .
> He will not fail or be discouraged
> till he has established justice in the earth;
> and the coastlands wait for his law.

In Isaiah 63:7-9 we also find the vision of God's Spirit at work in the long and turbulent history of Israel.

> I will recount the steadfast love of the LORD,
> the praises of the LORD,
> according to all that the LORD has granted us,
> and the great goodness to the house of Israel. . . .
> For he said, Surely they are my people. . . .
> In all their affliction he was afflicted,
> and the angel of his presence saved them;
> in his love and in his pity he redeemed them;
> he lifted them up and carried them all the days of old.

Though the people "rebelled and grieved his holy Spirit" (63:10), God remembered the days of old, the days of Moses and the Exodus, and again was revealed as the Father and Redeemer of Israel.

In Isaiah 63:10-11 we find two of the three places in the

Old Testament where the words *Holy Spirit* are used together. The only other reference is in Psalm 51:11.

As important as anything in the Old Testament is the promise of the future outpouring of the Spirit upon the people. The Spirit of God inspired the writers to look for the Messiah (see Isaiah 11:1-2). The Spirit of God will make the bones of the dead (referring to Israel in captivity to Babylon) come to life (Ezekiel 37:1-4). So the Lord said to Ezekiel: "And I will put my Spirit within you, and you shall live" (37:14). The Spirit will be poured out upon the house of Israel (39:29).

The prophet Joel gave this promise its supreme utterance in the Old Testament. He envisioned the outpouring of the Spirit on *all* people. He prophesied:

> And it shall come to pass afterward,
>   that I will pour out my spirit on all flesh;
> your sons and daughters shall prophesy,
>   your old men shall dream dreams,
>   and your young men shall see visions. (2:28)

Joel added: "And it shall come to pass that all who call upon the name of the LORD shall be delivered" (verse 32). Joel thus prepared the way for the later Christian understanding that all people who opened their lives to God would be filled with the Holy Spirit.

Importance for Our Spiritual Renewal

The main point to remember about the Old Testament teaching on the Spirit is that the Spirit of God took the initiative to be involved continuously in nature and in the lives of people. God is not some far-off, unconcerned deity who exists in the serene atmosphere of unconcern.

The God of the Old Testament not only created the universe and human beings, but also cares for all creatures. Indeed, in relation to both nature and human beings, God is *affected* by the misuse of nature and by wrong living. God actually suffers because of our misuse of natural resources and because of our sins. God suffers and is profoundly

15

dissatisfied with our defiance. The idea that God has no feeling, no wrath, no compassion is contrary to the teaching of the Old Testament.

God acted through the prophets and others to warn us and to *show* us that he will never forsake humanity. God has revealed a determination to use human history as a base of operations. God is the active, dynamic, energizing Spirit who is headed toward the Kingdom. And God is summoning the people of Israel to come along.

Therefore, on the basis of the revelation in the Old Testament, we can be sure that God cares for us. In addition, God makes demands of us, challenges us, and is eager to take the initiative to help us in our daily living. And God gives us many great promises with which we can face the future confidently.

God is mysteriously and wonderfully affected by the universe and by its creatures. We are told that after each stage of God's creative activity, God saw that what he did was good (Genesis 1:4, 10, 12, 18, 21, 25). After creating human beings, God looked upon them, and upon all that he had made, "and behold, it was very good" (1:31). The creatures God made—and the whole of creation—brought God great pleasure and satisfaction.

How is all this related to our spiritual renewal? First of all, this general perspective on God's caring concern for us made a profound contribution to the devotional literature of Israel. We can see why idolatry was forbidden in Israel. No statues of God were permitted. How can a statue of the dynamic, energizing, acting, caring God be created? Who can carve or form a statue of the living God?

The psalmists, more than any others, have taught us how to sing praises and give thanks to God. They knew that God delighted in humanity's faithfulness (see Psalms 19–34; 100; 103; and so forth).

The psalmists knew also that God is hurt to the depths when people do evil and disobey (see, for example, Psalms 1:4-6; 2:11; 5:4-6; 9:5-6; 37:10-20; 53:2-4). They knew also that *God reacts* to the expressed needs and prayers of people (Psalm 37:5; 55:22; 91:1-11; and so forth).

This understanding of the Spirit of God in the Old

Testament moves us toward pleasing, obeying, and glorifying God; for our deepest sense of joy and fulfillment comes from God's love and power. In God's purpose for us we find the true purpose for ourselves.

Thus the Old Testament laid the foundation on which the later understanding of the Spirit was built. And in a wonderful way it teaches us today to become intimately related to our Creator and Sustainer. Each of us has within a mysterious longing to know and love the One who made us. We long for this, we pray for this. And the vision of God given us through the inspired writers of the Old Testament enables us to behold the glory and presence of God.

In the Old Testament we are made aware of how God meets us at the point of our deepest needs, in the depths of loneliness and despair, in the times of pain and grief and tragedy for which we have no adequate language.

> Out of the depths I cry to thee, O LORD!
>   Lord, hear my voice!
> Let thy ears be attentive
>   to the voice of my supplications!
> (Psalm 130:1-2)

Finally, we learn from the Old Testament that sometimes God acts in unexpected ways to bless us. The Spirit of God works through the natural order, but is not limited to the sphere of natural laws. These laws have been established by God. They are steadfast ordinances. Beyond that, God moves into our lives with blessings—often surprising—out of God's vast supernatural resources.

CHAPTER 2

The Holy Spirit in the Four Gospels

We have seen that the Old Testament teaches that the Spirit of God is continuously dealing with us. This teaching is of utmost importance for vitally experienced religion. In addition, it prepares the way for the later understanding of the Holy Spirit that awaited the coming of Jesus Christ.

In the Birth of Jesus

The Synoptic Gospels (Matthew, Mark, and Luke) are concerned primarily with Jesus and not with the Holy Spirit. Yet the Holy Spirit is seen as dynamically at work in the birth and life of Jesus. In fact, in these Gospels we begin to see the connection between the Holy Spirit and Jesus.

According to Matthew and Luke, the Holy Spirit acted in the conception of Jesus (Matthew 1:18, 20; Luke 1:35). The Holy Spirit took the initiative in a special way, for a tremendously important purpose, to begin the new era of the kingdom of God through Jesus Christ.

The Holy Spirit filled Zechariah, the father of John the Baptist, so that he prophesied about John, saying: "And you, child, will be called the prophet of the Most High; / for you will go before the Lord to prepare his ways" (Luke 1:76).

Similarly, when Elizabeth, herself with child, saw Mary, she was filled with the Holy Spirit and exclaimed in a loud voice: "Blessed are you among women, and blessed is the fruit of your womb!" (Luke 1:42).

Again, the Holy Spirit came upon Simeon, a devout man in Jerusalem, and revealed to him that he would not die until he had seen the Christ. Inspired by the Spirit, Simeon went into the Temple and there saw Joseph and Mary with the child Jesus. Then he took the child in his arms and blessed God, saying: "Lord, now lettest thou thy servant depart in peace, / according to thy word; / for mine eyes have seen thy salvation" (Luke 2:29-30).

Therefore, from the start the inspired writers were telling us that the supernatural action of the Holy Spirit was at work in the coming of Jesus into the world.

In the Life of Jesus

The Holy Spirit acted also in special ways in the life of Jesus.

The Spirit descended upon Jesus like a dove at his baptism (Matthew 3:16; Mark 1:10). At that moment a voice from heaven said: "Thou art my beloved Son; with thee I am well pleased" (Mark 1:11).

It is interesting to note the difference between the Spirit's work in relation to John the Baptist and Jesus. In the case of John, the Holy Spirit simply carried forward the preparatory work of the Old Testament prophets. For John was the last in the line of those led by the Spirit to prepare the way for the Messiah. So it was no accident that Luke referred to the words of Isaiah in connection with John's mission: "The voice of one crying in the wilderness: / Prepare the way of the Lord" (3:4).

John himself knew that this was his mission. When people asked whether he was the Christ, he replied: "I baptize you with water; but he who is mightier than I is coming, the thong of whose sandals I am unworthy to untie; he will baptize you with the Holy Spirit and with fire" (Luke 3:16).

The inspired writers of Matthew, Mark, and Luke made clear in their writings that the work of the Holy Spirit could not be separated from the mission of Jesus Christ as the Savior of the world.

The Spirit was present with Jesus when he was tempted in the wilderness (Mark 1:12-13; see also Matthew 4:1; Luke 4:1). Jesus' temptations were real and fierce. He was tempted as we are (Hebrews 4:15) and even more strongly. And he was victorious. John Milton rightly said in his *Paradise Regained* that unless our Lord had won the victory during those forty days in the wilderness, there would have been no Gethsemane, Calvary, or Easter.

Jesus returned to Galilee in "the power of the Spirit." And the people were greatly moved and blessed by his work among them (Luke 4:14-15). Jesus "rejoiced in the Holy Spirit" when the seventy returned from their evangelistic mission (Luke 10:21). And evidently the earliest Christians were of one mind with Peter who said to Cornelius, "You know . . . how God anointed Jesus of Nazareth with the Holy Spirit and with power; how he went about doing good and healing all who were oppressed by the devil, for God was with him" (Acts 10:36, 38).

And Jesus himself was aware of the presence of the Spirit with him in his marvelous ministry to the poor, the captives, the blind, and the oppressed (Luke 4:18-21). Thus the Holy Spirit moved through him with compassionate concern for justice and liberation for the needy.

What Jesus Taught About the Holy Spirit

From ancient times John's Gospel has been called the spiritual Gospel. All of the Gospels are spiritual, but in the Fourth Gospel there are certain special emphases on Jesus as the Word of God, the Bread of life, the Light of the world, the Good Shepherd, the Way, the Truth, and the Life, and the One through whom the Holy Spirit would come. Nevertheless, a careful study of this Gospel reveals a profound interest in the historical Jesus, that is, in what Jesus said and did (see 20:30-31; 21:24-25).

Some of the incidents recorded in John are not found in any of the other three Gospels, such as the biblical accounts of Jesus and Nicodemus (3:1-15), Jesus and the Samaritan woman (4:1-26), Jesus and the man born blind (Chapter 9), Jesus and the woman caught in adultery (8:3-11).

In addition, a major concern of the author was to help us understand Jesus as the One sent from God to be the life-giving Word of God, the Savior of the world, and the Inaugurator of a new era of the grace of God through the power of the Holy Spirit.

In John's Gospel, even when the Holy Spirit is not referred to explicitly, preparatory incidents and statements open the door to the promised new era of the Holy Spirit. In the very first few verses, the whole realm of the supernatural is laid out as the basis of all that is to follow.

> In the beginning was the Word, and the Word was with God, and the Word was God. He was in the beginning with God; all things were made through him, and without him was not anything made that was made. In him was life, and the life was the light of men. The light shines in the darkness, and the darkness has not overcome it [or did not comprehend it]. (1:1-5)

In the Fourth Gospel we find a remarkable witness of John the Baptist to Jesus as the Christ. As John baptized Jesus, John said: "I saw the Spirit descend as a dove from heaven, and it remained on him" (John 1:32). For God had told John the Baptist: "He on whom you see the Spirit descend and remain, this is he who baptizes with the Holy Spirit" (verse 33). So John the Baptist was given to see and proclaim that Jesus is the Son of God (verse 34).

Another preparatory scene in this Gospel is that of Jesus and Nicodemus (3:1-15). Here the wondrous energy of the Spirit is understood to be at work in the new birth. Jesus speaks of the mystery of the Spirit's wonderworking power. That power is like the coming and going of the wind whose origin and end we cannot see. There is in what Jesus said the mysterious supernatural power whereby a soul is born of the Spirit. "That which is born of the flesh is flesh, and that which is born of the Spirit is spirit" (verse 6). Jesus referred also to God's *measureless* gift of the Spirit (verse 34).

The Master was speaking of the same Source of power when he said to the Samaritan woman, "whoever drinks of the water that I shall give him will never thirst; the water that I shall give him will become in him a spring of water welling up to eternal life" (4:14). Closely related to this is what Jesus said of those who come to him for spiritual water. "Out of his heart will flow rivers of living water" (7:38).

The most important teachings of Jesus on the Holy Spirit are found in John 14–16. In Chapter 14, the disciples are told that God will send "another Counselor" (verse 16), "even the Spirit of truth, whom the world cannot receive, because it neither sees him nor knows him; you know him, for he dwells with you, and will be in you" (verse 17). But the promise requires obedience to the Lord's commandments. Then Jesus went on to say, "These things I have spoken to you, while I am still with you. But the Counselor, the Holy Spirit, whom the Father will send in my name, he will teach you all things, and bring to your remembrance all that I have said to you" (14:25-26).

In John 15, Jesus refers to himself as the "true vine." His followers are the branches that cannot live and bear fruit unless they abide in him. "For," as Jesus said, "apart from me you can do nothing" (verse 5). The Master's great concern here is that his followers obey his commandments, "bear much fruit" in the Kingdom, and experience the great fullness of joy in the Lord (verses 7-11). In this way the followers of Jesus will receive the Holy Spirit, obey the commandment of love, and, in spite of persecution, bear witness to Jesus as the Savior of the world (15:12-27).

The teaching of Jesus on the Holy Spirit in John 16 is even more explicit than in the two preceding chapters. Here Jesus identified with finality the ever-present connection between the Holy Spirit's mission and his own. In verses 7-15 we find what is perhaps the greatest passage on the Holy Spirit in the Gospels. Jesus wanted to prepare his disciples for the fact that his earthly mission was to come to an end. What were they to do? How could they go on? So Jesus said:

> Nevertheless I tell you the truth: it is to your advantage that I go away, for if I do not go away, the Counselor will not come to you; but if I go, I will send him to you. And when he comes, he will convince the world concerning sin and righteousness and judgment; concerning sin, because they do not believe in me; concerning righteousness, because I go to the Father, and you

will see me no more; concerning judgment, because the ruler of this world is judged.

I have yet many things to say to you, but you cannot bear them now. When the Spirit of truth comes, he will guide you into all the truth; for he will not speak on his own authority, but whatever he hears he will speak, and he will declare to you the things that are to come. He will glorify me, for he will take what is mine and declare it to you. All that the Father has is mine; therefore I said that he will take what is mine and declare it to you.

This passage contains at least five important thoughts. First, the coming of the Holy Spirit in full power had to wait for Jesus' earthly mission to be completed. "If I do not go away," said Jesus, "the Counselor will not come to you." This requirement was suggested earlier in John's Gospel: "Now this he said about the Spirit, which those who believed in him were to receive; for as yet the Spirit had not been given, because Jesus was not yet glorified" (7:39).

Second, Jesus made it clear that he was the one who would send the Holy Spirit through the Father. In substance, this is the same as praying to the Father to send the Spirit (14:16). The Holy Spirit was to convince the world of sin, to proclaim righteousness, and to make people aware of the judgment of God. Here the implication is that just as Jesus did these things during his earthly ministry, so the Holy Spirit will continue to do them by lifting up Jesus Christ in the world.

Third, this passage (16:7-15) clearly states that the Holy Spirit's unique mission is to magnify Jesus Christ. "He will glorify me, for he will take what is mine and declare it to you." This should be tied to the words, "he will guide you into all the truth." When the Holy Spirit is spoken of as the "Spirit of truth," this does not refer to philosophical, scientific, or historical truth. The Holy Spirit does not function as an encyclopedia or as a course in science or in reflective thinking. Rather, the Holy Spirit will guide people into *all the truth they need for their salvation in Jesus Christ*. The Holy Spirit will glorify Jesus Christ. And the statement that "he will declare to you the things that are to come" would seem to refer, among other things, to the ultimate triumph of righteousness under the lordship of Jesus Christ.

Fourth, the work of the Holy Spirit does not proclaim the Holy Spirit. The Spirit comes bearing Jesus' message. The Holy Spirit "will take what is mine," said Jesus, "and declare it to you" (verse 14). The one great concern of the Holy Spirit is the new era of the kingdom of God in and through Jesus Christ.

Fifth, the Holy Spirit magnifies Jesus Christ in his *teaching* ministry: *communicating* who Jesus was; what his message was; and what his life, death, and resurrection mean in the inauguration of God's new era.

The directives here are clear. Jesus himself made it forever impossible to separate the mission of the Holy Spirit from his own great work as Lord and Savior.

The Promise of the Outpouring of the Spirit

The risen Lord promised his disciples that they would be provided with "power from on high" (Luke 24:49) so their minds could truly grasp that Jesus was the One written about "in the law of Moses and the prophets and the psalms" (verse 44). In addition, they were to stay in Jerusalem until they received power from on high so they could become effective witnesses to God's great salvation in Jesus Christ (verse 49). Those who preach and teach Christ will suffer and be sorely tried. They cannot do their work without the "power from on high" promised by the risen Lord.

Again, in the Book of Acts we are given the risen Savior's promise. He said that his disciples were to "wait for the promise of the Father, which, he said, 'you heard from me, for John baptized with water, but before many days you shall be baptized with the Holy Spirit' " (1:4-5). Then he continued: "But you shall receive power when the Holy Spirit has come upon you; and you shall be my witnesses in Jerusalem and in all Judea and Samaria and to the end of the earth" (verse 8).

Importance for Our Spiritual Renewal

As we have seen, the mission of the Holy Spirit is to carry forward the mission of Jesus Christ and his kingdom. To that end the Spirit brings conviction of sin, assists us to repent and to put our trust in the Savior, helps us pray earnestly for the Kingdom, and empowers us for mission and effective service.

Manifestly this mission is related to our spiritual life, to the life of prayer, effective living, and service. Consider two supportive thoughts.

First, it is marvelous that in the four Gospels God has revealed this mysterious connection between Jesus Christ and the Holy Spirit. Think what happens in our spiritual life when we let other things crowd out Jesus Christ. I know some persons who speak so much of the Holy Spirit, of "Spirit baptism," of being "full of the Spirit," that we wonder when they last thought of Jesus. They experience hunches as coming from the Spirit. They entertain expectations as received from the Spirit. They may hear voices, see visions, or feel impulses that make them believe they and not others have an inside track to God. And they cannot remember when they last thought of Jesus or read the four Gospels or even the Sermon on the Mount.

Let me make myself clear here. The Holy Spirit may be the instrument of authentic visions, significant expectations, experiences of divine guidance, and healings in body and mind. But we must understand that all of these are coming to us through the presence and power of the living Christ.

The primary clue to the spiritual life and power is to begin by meditating on Jesus, on what he said and did, and on his living presence with us now where we are. The Holy Spirit helps us do this as we read the four Gospels. And mysteriously, we begin to feel the presence of the living Christ and the surging "power from on high."

Second, we see in the light of this why, in the spiritual formation of people in the church, we keep returning to Jesus Christ, the crucified and risen Lord: Jesus is the center of our worship and "the pioneer and perfecter of our faith" (Hebrews 12:2).

CHAPTER 3

Pentecost and Paul

Next in importance to what we find in the four Gospels are these two sources on the Holy Spirit: (1) the happenings at Pentecost and following; and (2) the inspired remarks of the apostle Paul.

We find the primary references on Pentecost and its aftermath in Acts 2, as well as in the entire Book of Acts. The major references to the witness and teaching of Paul are to be found in selected passages of the Book of Acts and in Romans, Chapter 8; 1 Corinthians, Chapters 12–14; and in various references in his other letters. We turn to these now, beginning with Pentecost.

Pentecost and Following

Most people who read about the first Christian Pentecost are likely to start with the first four verses of Acts 2. While those verses are of utmost importance, the whole chapter is necessary in order to understand the deeper dimensions of what has been called an eternal moment in the destiny of humankind. We shall begin with Acts 2:1-4 and then move on to other key verses in the chapter.

At first we are struck with the unusual happenings. "Suddenly a sound came from heaven like the rush of a mighty wind, and it filled all the house where they were sitting. And there appeared to them tongues as of fire, distributed and resting on each one of them. And they were all filled with the Holy Spirit and began to speak in other tongues" (verses 2-4).

Were these events all that happened? Were they the deepest dimensions of the experience of those earliest Christians at Pentecost? The answer has to be no to both questions. To be sure, those outward signs were important. They served as confirming signs of the extraordinary presence and power of the Holy Spirit. That particular moment in history, in a true sense, marked the *real beginning of the community of faith* that was ever afterward to bear the name of Jesus Christ.

When we read further into Acts and notice what Peter said, we begin to see the deeper meaning of Pentecost.

Who was this Peter? Remember that even though he may have said to Jesus, "You are the Christ, the Son of the living God" (Matthew 16:16), he did not really understand or deeply believe what he was saying. Jesus said to him, "Blessed are you, Simon Bar-Jona! For flesh and blood has not revealed this to you, but my Father who is in heaven" (verse 17). Still, Peter did not grasp the full import of what he had said. How do we know this? We know it because later, in the presence of a servant girl, at a time when Jesus Christ was being persecuted, Peter denied that he had anything to do with Jesus (Matthew 26:59-75). In other words, when Jesus was arrested, mocked, and tortured, Peter denied him three times.

But now look at that same man after the outpouring of the Holy Spirit at Pentecost. A vast multitude had gathered, possibly in the Temple area. Those who had received the outpouring of the Holy Spirit with Peter were there with him. And he stood forth to speak. The magnificent setting of the Temple area, with its massive colonnades, would have made a most impressive background for what Peter had to say. In this area Jesus' crucifixion had been plotted. Not far away was the place where Peter had trembled and in cowardice denied his Lord.

Peter now lifted up his voice and addressed the multitude. What did he say? He said that what the prophet

Joel had predicted about the outpouring of the Spirit had become a reality (Acts 2:17-21). He went on to talk about Jesus, his life, death, and resurrection (verses 22-24). He tied all this into what David had said (verses 25-31). Then he spoke of Jesus' apostles as witnesses to the risen Lord and to the fact that through this exalted Lord the Holy Spirit had been poured out on his followers (verses 32-33). Peter gave this extraordinary witness: "Let all the house of Israel therefore know assuredly that God has made him both Lord and Christ, this Jesus whom you crucified" (verse 36).

When the people asked, "Brethren, what shall we do?" Peter said, "Repent and be baptized every one of you in the name of Jesus Christ for the forgiveness of your sins; and you shall receive the gift of the Holy Spirit" (verse 38). We may note that he did not say there would be the rushing of a mighty wind or "tongues as of fire" resting on them, nor did he promise that they would speak in "other tongues." He simply said that through repentance, baptism, and faith in Jesus' name they would receive the gift of the Holy Spirit. He made no mention of specific outer signs. This does not mean that he did not consider them important. Rather, he was lifting up the primary reality of what had taken place.

One thing is sure: Peter was speaking to a multitude of people, most of whom already knew something of Jesus through his teachings and mighty deeds among them. Some had heard him preach; some had been healed by him or were relatives of people who had been healed by him. Some had been in the mob that cried for Barabbas and said, "Away with this man!" "Crucify him!" (Luke 23:18, 21). This band of Christians experienced the presence and power of God through their crucified and risen Lord. But this experience became a reality in their hearts through the power of the Holy Spirit. It seems clear that the Holy Spirit first illuminated their minds so that they grasped for the first time, in any settled way, the revealed truth that Jesus Christ was indeed the God-appointed Savior of the world and the Inaugurator of the new era of the kingdom of God. The Spirit of truth had opened their minds to comprehend the one indispensable reality. After that threats of prison or torture or persecution could not deter Peter and the others. Their commitment was sealed; they were filled with the power of the Holy Spirit.

Let us get the full picture. In Acts 2:1 we read: "When the day of Pentecost had come, they were all together in one place." Who were "they"? This point is important, for the Holy Spirit did not act indiscriminately. But the moment we ask who were gathered together at that first Christian outpouring of the Spirit, we know who they were. *They were persons who had been with Jesus.* They shared a holy memory of what Jesus had said and done. One of them might have said, "Do you remember when He told us, 'I am the Light of the world'?" Then someone would add, "Yes, and remember when He said, 'You are the light of the world'?" One after another may have repeated some saying or referred to an incident. "You remember Zacchaeus?" "Yes, and what about blind Bartimaeus?" "You remember the story of the prodigal son?" "And the parable of the sower?" "Oh, and what He prayed in agony on the cross!" So on and on it went.

The Holy Spirit stirred up and quickened their common memory with so many of Jesus' sayings and deeds that they were prepared to receive their risen Lord into their hearts. He was the supreme reality in their midst. The world was pushed into the background and Jesus was magnified.

Add to this a vivid awareness of Jesus' resurrection. They were the ones who shared the holy memory of Jesus as he had suffered and died only a few days before. They also were the ones who saw the empty tomb and who beheld again and again their risen Lord. Jesus was alive. Risen! They had seen and heard for themselves. These clues, among others, lead us to the overarching conclusion that that group of people—and that group only—was prepared to receive the power of the Holy Spirit at that eternal moment in the destiny of humankind.

The people at that first Christian Pentecost also shared a common understanding of who Jesus was in the light of Old Testament Scripture. These people, and this was true later of Paul, interpreted Jesus as the promised Messiah. They understood that Jesus did not come into the world like a bolt out of the blue. His coming had been preceded by long centuries of preparation through the history and prophets of Israel. God, in his infinite love and wisdom, had acted in their time to mark the beginning of the new era of the kingdom of God. Paul, though not present in that group, caught its spirit later when he said, "But when the time had fully come, God sent forth his Son" (Galatians 4:4).

We need to underscore one more factor. Those who shared in that outpouring had heard Jesus promise them the Holy Spirit. This was significant not merely because Jesus had made this promise prior to his crucifixion, but it was significant also because the risen Lord himself promised it again. They had heard his great commission to be his witnesses in Jerusalem and in all Judea and Samaria and to the end of the earth (Acts 1:8). But they were not to go until they had received the "power from on high." Therefore, the atmosphere was charged with expectancy. They were all filled with the Holy Spirit.

The Teaching of Paul

When we come to what Paul said on the Holy Spirit, no single passage will do. We need to look at selected passages from his letters and also at certain emphases in his teachings and in his life as a Christian leader. Above all, we need to remember that the most important event in the background of Paul's life as a Christian was his encounter with the risen Lord on the road to Damascus.

Paul had a genius for going to the point. In writing to the Christians at Corinth he said, "No one can say 'Jesus is Lord' except by the Holy Spirit" (1 Corinthians 12:3). The words, *Jesus is Lord,* formed one of the earliest confessions of faith. Paul was reminding the Corinthian Christians that no one can truly say those words without the assistance of the Holy Spirit.

At times Paul came very close to identifying the Holy Spirit with the spirit of the risen Christ. He said, "Now the Lord is the Spirit, and where the Spirit of the Lord is, there is freedom. And we all, with unveiled face, beholding the glory of the Lord, are being changed into his likeness from one degree of glory to another; for this comes from the Lord who is the Spirit" (2 Corinthians 3:17-18).

Earlier in this book we saw that Jesus made it impossible to separate the work of the Holy Spirit from his own mission as the Savior of the world and as the Inaugurator of the new era of the kingdom of God. In this chapter we have already seen that when we understand the deeper meaning of Pentecost, we find that the power of the Holy Spirit cannot be separated from the grace of God in Jesus Christ. Paul also taught that we cannot separate the work of the Holy Spirit from that of Jesus Christ as Lord and Redeemer. At the same time, in order to deal with division among the Corinthians, Paul shared with them some practical implications of the Holy Spirit's work in carrying forward the unique mission of Jesus Christ in the world.

Paul wrote more about his own experience as a Christian and his own interpretation of Christianity than any other writer in the New Testament. In addition to his explicit statements already mentioned, his words often *imply* thoughts on the Holy Spirit. His deep convictions on the Holy Spirit are reflected in his personal testimony about what Christ meant to him. For example, he said, "For I decided to know nothing among you except Jesus Christ and him crucified" (1 Corinthians 2:2). And again he said, "For to me to live is Christ, and to die is gain" (Philippians 1:21).

Paul was a remarkable example of how a Christian leader performs when filled with the Holy Spirit. His life tells us as much as his specific teachings on the Spirit. He shows us how the Spirit works in a gifted human being who is totally dedicated to Jesus Christ. We see in Paul what happens when the Holy Spirit re-creates a person to carry forward the Lord's work in the world. His ministry was one of creative leadership coupled with a spirit of humility, love, and reconciliation. He illustrates the fact that whenever the Holy Spirit is truly at work in a Christian, he or she is freed from divisiveness, bitterness, and an unforgiving spirit.

One magnificent theme that brings together everything Paul said on the Holy Spirit is but a further expression of what Jesus taught and what was confirmed at Pentecost.

That mighty theme is the centrality and finality of Jesus Christ as the Savior of the world. To Paul this theme was intimately personal. Jesus Christ was the basic reality of his existence as a Christian.

The number of Paul's references to Jesus Christ as Redeemer and Lord overwhelms the reader of his letters. For Paul everything depends on Jesus' life, death, and resurrection. Some people think of their own Christian experiences as the final ground of belief. Not so Paul. He knew the presence of the living Christ in his soul, but he proclaimed only the authority and finality of Jesus Christ crucified and raised from the dead. This reality, confirmed in experience, stands in its own right in the far-reaching providence of God. Paul never allowed his Christian experience to obscure the risen Lord who gave it to him.

For Paul, the Gospel was the good news of Jesus Christ. "For I delivered to you as of first importance what I also received, that Christ died for our sins in accordance with the scriptures" (1 Corinthians 15:3). Then Paul went on to speak of Jesus' resurrection and of his appearances to the disciples and others, including himself (verses 4-8). Though unworthy because he had persecuted the church, Paul was what he was by the grace of God (verses 9-10).

Paul believed profoundly in the affirmation that the new era of salvation by grace came into the world through Jesus Christ. He experienced this salvation in his own heart. And he proclaimed it as God's gift to all who would repent and have faith. In one of his finest and most familiar passages he said, "There is therefore now no condemnation for those who are in Christ Jesus. For the law of the Spirit of life in Christ Jesus has set me free from the law of sin and death" (Romans 8:1-2).

Again, Paul wrote to the Christians at Rome, "But you are not in the flesh, you are in the Spirit, if in fact the Spirit of God dwells in you. Any one who does not have the Spirit of Christ does not belong to him" (8:9). Paul interpreted Old Testament Scripture under the inspiration of the Holy Spirit. Consequently, he saw the Old Testament as preparing for the coming of Jesus Christ, the promised Messiah. Paul knew that God had revealed himself in wonderful ways in the Old Testament. But when it came to the proclamation of the gospel, Paul saw the glory of the Old Testament primarily in relation to Jesus Christ. Therefore, when he went about in his missionary work, Paul expounded upon Jesus as the Christ by using the Old Testament as a primary means of convincing people. He taught on the basis of Scripture that Jesus Christ was the promised Messiah and Savior of the world.

Paul emphasized that Christians are bound to one another as members of the body of Christ (1 Corinthians 12:12-31). The Holy Spirit moved Paul with the passion to create local churches. Just as the Spirit formed the church at Pentecost, so the Spirit continued to be concerned with keeping the gospel alive through Paul's determination to form and nurture local churches wherever he went. The letters to the various churches (at Corinth, Ephesus, Philippi, Thessalonica, in Rome, and Galatia) illustrate this determination. As we have seen, the Holy Spirit magnifies Jesus Christ by bringing people together in the unity of the Spirit.

In 1 Corinthians 12 and 14, Paul referred to certain special manifestations or gifts of the Spirit. He said, "To each is given the manifestation of the Spirit for the common good" (12:7).

Paul said that in the practical work of the church, the Holy Spirit moves through different individuals by means of special manifestations or gifts (verses 8-10). Each member of the body of Christ is important. Through each and all, the Holy Spirit binds Christians together in the living community of faith, whose sole foundation is Jesus Christ (1 Corinthians 3:11). All the manifestations or gifts of the Spirit "are inspired by one and the same Spirit, who apportions to each one individually as he wills" (12:11).

Paul went on to say, "For just as the body is one and has many members, and all the members of the body, though many, are one body, so it is with Christ" (verse 12).

Paul is teaching that the nature of the Holy Spirit is to bring into the body of Christ the spirit of love, patience, understanding, and cooperation (1 Corinthians 13). And the dynamics of the glorious experience of the Holy Spirit are not to lead to chaos or disorder in the local church (Chapter 14). On the one hand, Paul does not want the work of the Spirit to be stifled; the vitality must be there. At the same time, the vitality of the Spirit needs to be tempered by the same Spirit's movement toward order. The most important point here is that the work of the Spirit is to magnify Jesus Christ and carry forward his work through the cooperative interaction of all the members that bear his name.

Above all, Paul wanted the Christians at Corinth to emphasize what he called "the higher gifts" (12:31). That is why he said, "Make love your aim, and earnestly desire the spiritual gifts" (14:1). Elsewhere, Paul tells us that the fruit of the Spirit is "love, joy, peace, patience, kindness, goodness, faithfulness, gentleness, self-control" (Galatians 5:22-23). The basic point is that the Holy Spirit gives us the Christlike spirit. All other manifestations or gifts further that supreme gift of the living Christ in us.

Importance for Our Spiritual Renewal

In the marvelous light of Pentecost and of what Paul taught, we see at least four things of utmost importance for our spiritual renewal.

First, we find our souls drawn to Jesus Christ. We have already referred to this in the preceding chapter. But that vision is now confirmed and amplified by Pentecost and by Paul's teaching. We feel the Holy Spirit working in us, as at Pentecost, to draw us closer to Jesus Christ. And when we know that Jesus Christ is the Lord of our lives *now*, we feel the surging power of his presence as he controls our tempers, rules our tongues, and floods our souls with his love. We feel his presence, through the Holy Spirit, as he gives us *now* the power to break destructive habits, to rise about tough situations, to go through life's storms.

Second, in the light of Pentecost and Paul's teaching, we are moved into the dynamic experience of prayer in the name of Jesus. This prayer is for those we love, lifting them up to God in faith that they may be redeemed and made whole in body, mind, and spirit. The Holy Spirit moves us to pray for those who in the name of Jesus Christ and his justice are suffering in prison or in various kinds of persecution. This kind of prayer binds all together in the body of Christ. And it moves whole churches into a marvelous newfound spirit of forgiveness, love, and unity.

Third, from Pentecost and Paul we learn that the Holy Spirit may come into our souls suddenly in special ways. A whole church may be awakened by some sudden outpouring of the Spirit. Then we shall see special manifestations willed by the Spirit. Therefore, we should have a sense of expectancy. For the Spirit ever seeks to bless us and to give us the supernatural help under Christ which we must have in order to see life through.

Fourth, we learn from Pentecost and the teaching of Paul that the Holy Spirit provides the only adequate motivation for carrying out the world mission of Jesus Christ. This mission goes far deeper than the worthy concern for world peace, for the conquest of poverty, and for health of body and mind, although it includes all of those. In addition, the Holy Spirit moves Christians to draw all people to the Creator who made them and who claims them. The Spirit motivates them to enter into a life-giving faith relationship with God through Jesus Christ. From all this motivation must flow those efforts and deeds that meet the crying needs of human beings everywhere.

CHAPTER 4

The Holy Spirit and the Church

Jesus formed his disciples into a community of prayer and faith. But until the day of Pentecost, they did not have the inner resources necessary for carrying forward the work of the Lord. They had walked with Jesus. They had sat at his feet and learned from him. They had watched him in his healing ministry, and they had participated in significant activities of preaching and healing when Jesus sent them out. They witnessed his crucifixion from afar. All of them, along with many others, had seen the risen Christ and had heard his teaching and instructions. The risen Christ appeared to them during a period of forty days and taught them concerning the kingdom of God (Acts 1:3). They heard the Master's charge to "go therefore and make disciples of all nations, baptizing them in the name of the Father and of the Son and of the Holy Spirit" (Matthew 28:19). They were filled with anticipation because of the promise of their risen Lord that they were to receive power when the Holy Spirit would come upon them (Acts 1:8).

Then came Pentecost. What happened at Pentecost that was related particularly to the ongoing life of the community of prayer and faith, that is, of the church?

We have seen that the Holy Spirit is at work in the various stages of Christian experience. In other words, the Spirit is dynamically present in every human being and, in special ways, in the ongoing lives of Christians. In addition, the Holy Spirit is present in the community of prayer and faith that bears the name of Jesus Christ. The church is the body of Christ. Just what does the Holy Spirit do in the formation, nurture, and world outreach of the church? I would suggest at least five things. (1) The Holy Spirit binds Christians together into a supportive fellowship of prayer and faith. (2) The Holy Spirit is actively present in the church to preserve the identity and integrity of the gospel. (3) The Holy Spirit calls some persons to proclaim the gospel, to teach the Word, and to administer the sacraments. (4) The Holy Spirit summons all Christians to responsible living in community. (5) The Holy Spirit calls upon all Christians to join together in the great mission of world evangelization. Let us consider these points in that order.

The Holy Spirit Binds Christians Together

The Holy Spirit binds Christians together in local churches and small groups for supportive fellowship. We sing, "Blest be the tie that binds / our hearts in Christian love" (*The Book of Hymns*, Number 306). What is that tie? It is the power and presence of the Holy Spirit. The Holy Spirit moves us to pray for one another and to strengthen one another in the faith and in practical Christian living.

Ever since the days of the earliest churches, there have been differences within them. Paul had to deal with this situation in the church at Corinth as well as the one in Galatia. The church is imperfect because it is made up of imperfect human beings. Nevertheless, we are bound to one another through Jesus Christ our crucified and risen Lord. Through the power of the Holy Spirit we share together in the ministry of intercessory prayer for one another and for all persons we know to be in need. This intercessory prayer, of course, necessarily expresses itself in service.

People said that the earliest Christians loved one another. Through this love they became living answers to the prayer of Jesus for the unity of all his followers (John 17). Paul likened the church to the physical body. He pointed out that we have different abilities and different manifestations of the Spirit for the common good. But we are all united in Christ. "For just as the body is one and has many members, and all the members of the body, though many, are one body, so it is with Christ. For by one Spirit we were all baptized into one body—Jews or Greeks, slaves or free—and all were made to drink of one Spirit" (1 Corinthians 12:12-13).

So the Holy Spirit binds us together into a living, supportive fellowship of prayer and faith as members of the body of Christ. Each of us needs a support system. The Holy Spirit provides this support through a Christian family life. The Holy Spirit provides it also through small prayer-study-service groups in the church. The Holy Spirit makes this support system available in the experiences of public worship and in the cooperative deeds that flow from prayer and worship.

The Holy Spirit and the Integrity of the Gospel

The Holy Spirit works in the church to preserve the integrity of the gospel. The greatest and most precious treasure of the church is the gospel of salvation in Jesus Christ. Salvation is the power of God whereby we are forgiven and re-created for effective and adventurous living in the kingdom of God while we are on this earth. This gospel is also the basis for our eternal salvation. Therefore, the Holy Spirit has been continuously working within the body of Christ to preserve the gospel.

This gospel, this good news, alone answers the deepest questions of the human spirit. How can I be forgiven? Where can I find the power to be what God wants me to be? What is the meaning or purpose of my life? After death, what?

If we want to be free from guilt, to be forgiven, where are we to go? Shall we go to the scientific laboratories in the great universities? Of course not. If we do not go to the foot of the cross, where?

If we want to be empowered for effective living, for

victory over temptation and over destructive habits, where are we to go? Are we to go to science, to technology, to computers? Of course not. We know that we are to return again and again to Jesus Christ our Savior and Lord who, through the power of the Holy Spirit, ever lives within our souls to bless us and empower us for creative living.

If we want to know the answer to the question of the meaning of life, where shall we go? To philosophers, to the worldly-wise, to modern culture and civilization? Of course not. We return to the Bible and to the gospel, which is the power of God unto salvation. Through the gospel we find a new meaning and glory in our lives on this earth.

And what about death? Shall we turn to computers? Or to diets and exercises? Or shall we turn to the two thousand or more people in the United States of America who claim to be messiahs?

In one fascinating scene in the Bible Jesus made some strong statements to people and many of his followers drew back and went away from him. Jesus then said to the twelve, "Do you also wish to go away?" And Simon Peter answered him, "Lord, to whom shall we go? You have the words of eternal life" (John 6:67-68). We join Simon Peter in asking the question: If not to Jesus Christ, to whom shall we go? How does the Holy Spirit work in the church to preserve the integrity of the gospel? I suggest some ways:

1. The Holy Spirit illuminates the Bible so we understand it through the eyes of faith. The Holy Spirit inspires ministers to an ever-growing and ever-deepening understanding of the Bible as the revealed Word of God. In addition, through Sunday school classes and Bible study groups, the Holy Spirit illuminates the minds of lay persons, helping them to grow in their understanding of the Bible and of the promises of God in Jesus Christ.

2. The Holy Spirit has worked in the church, and continues to do so, through the great creedal affirmations. These creeds are efforts in the ongoing life of the church to summarize what the biblical revelation is all about. They lift up the doctrines and emphases that are at the heart of the gospel.

3. Again, the Holy Spirit is working in the life of the

church through the sacraments of Baptism and the Lord's Supper. In the orders of service for these two sacraments, we have profound statements concerning the nature of the gospel. The Holy Spirit has been at work in the development of these statements and continues to work in and through the community of prayer and faith to bring home the deeper meaning of the liturgies for Baptism and Holy Communion with their clear emphasis upon the gospel of salvation in Jesus Christ.

4. The Holy Spirit is at work in and through the great hymns. These hymns have been selected over a period of many centuries by Christian leaders who felt that somehow the Holy Spirit had inspired them. They tell the story of salvation in Jesus Christ and emphasize the true nature of the gospel and the purpose of God in making salvation available in Jesus Christ.

5. Once more, the Holy Spirit has confirmed the truth and power of the gospel through the testimony and lives of outstanding Christians in local churches. The Holy Spirit has taught them to see that we are not forgiven and empowered by our own deeds, by culture, by civilization, by computers, or by science, but by the grace of God (Ephesians 2:8). Therefore, through these witnesses in all of our local churches, the Holy Spirit has moved to identify and maintain the integrity of the gospel of salvation in Jesus Christ.

The Holy Spirit and Those Called to the Ministry

The Holy Spirit calls some persons to devote their lives to preaching the gospel, to teaching the Bible, to administering the sacraments, and to being the spiritual leaders in the body of Christ. In the Old Testament God chose certain people for moral and spiritual leadership. Those chosen were Abraham, Moses, David, and the prophets. Jesus chose the twelve. The risen Lord commissioned the disciples and chose Saul of Tarsus. All through history, through the Holy Spirit, God has called people to lead in communicating the gospel so the church could go forward. Our own heritage includes Susanna Wesley, John and Charles Wesley, Francis Asbury, Harry Hosier, Jacob Albright, Philip William Otterbein, and the circuit riders.

Clearly, God's administrative policy has been and continues to be the calling of certain persons to do the great work of proclaiming the gospel of our Lord and Savior Jesus Christ. This call has come to people through the presence and inspiration of the Holy Spirit. Those who are called belong in a long succession of persons going back to the apostles.

We know that unless some people are called of God and set apart through the church for the ministry, Christ's work will not be carried forward effectively. Paul knew this when he said, "But how are men to call upon him in whom they have not believed? And how are they to believe in him of whom they have never heard? And how are they to hear without a preacher? And how can men preach unless they are sent? As it is written, 'How beautiful are the feet of those who preach good news!' " (Romans 10:14-15).

The Holy Spirit is at work in the church in this process when, after careful examination and prayer, the church recognizes the authenticity of the call to the ministry and ordains those who are called. Those who are called experience the sense of awe, of mystery, of inadequacy, and of the desire to do their best for the Lord. And they always have a profound awareness of the need for prayer and for the continuing presence of the risen Christ through the power of the Holy Spirit.

The Holy Spirit Calls Us
to Responsible Living in Community

The Holy Spirit moves in the hearts of believers within the community of prayer and faith by calling them to responsible living in community. Christians are not isolated from the world in which we live, and the Spirit moves in to help us reflect Christ's love in our deeds. The Holy Spirit is present not only in life's mountaintop experiences but also in the daily rounds of love and duty. The Spirit sustains and empowers us for responsible living in the workaday realms. The Spirit moves in us in our homes, our places of work, our recreation, our citizenship, and in our life together in the church.

The Holy Spirit and World Evangelization

We see the Holy Spirit's dynamic presence in the yearning of the community of prayer and faith to evangelize the world. This yearning is awakened through the presence of the Holy Spirit. Everyone needs the gospel. For the gospel is, as Paul said, "the power of God for salvation to every one who has faith" (Romans 1:16).

A most amazing evidence of the activity of the Holy Spirit following that first Pentecost was the power of those Christians to win others to Christ. Thousands were converted (Acts 2:41; 4:4; 5:14; 6:7). To be sure, many of these thousands had already been with Jesus. They had heard him preach and teach. They had seen his miracles. Indeed, many of them and many of their relatives had been healed by him. They were also aware of the Crucifixion. In addition, those who were filled with the Holy Spirit at Pentecost had been recently with their risen Lord. The event of the Resurrection filled their minds with a sense of the wonder, mystery, and glory of God's mighty supernatural action. The Holy Spirit turned the holy remembrance of these events, so fresh on their minds, into a dynamic source of witness. They witnessed to the glory of God in Jesus Christ with special emphasis on the resurrection.

This power from the Holy Spirit to help people witness for Jesus Christ was seen not only around Jerusalem but also at Antioch, where the followers of Jesus were first called Christians (Acts 11:26). A great number of people there believed in the Lord (Acts 11:21).

What was the source of this extraordinary power to win people for Jesus Christ in those days? His followers obeyed the command of Jesus to "stay in the city, until you are clothed with power from on high" (Luke 24:49). That is, through the power of the Holy Spirit, those early Christians in Jerusalem, Antioch, and elsewhere beheld the glory of what God had done in Jesus Christ. They recovered the vision of God's dealings with Moses and the prophets as recorded in the only Scriptures they had (what we call the Old Testament). They *experienced* the holy memory of Jesus' life, death, and resurrection. Through the Spirit they were given a holy awareness of the individual's desperate need for God's salvation. They saw people as creatures lost in the wastelands of sin, bad habits, despair, and death. Above all, they *experienced* with a new freshness the new life in Christ. They felt the inner working of a new power for righteousness by grace through faith. At the same time, they were given the vision of God's plan to carry forward the work of the Kingdom through Jesus Christ (see Ephesians 1:9-10). All this was made effective in their lives through the presence of the Holy Spirit.

In short, the evangelistic power of those earliest Christians was no accident. It came from waiting in Jerusalem and opening their souls to receive the power of the Holy Spirit from above. Therefore, they *had* to witness. They were moved by the Holy Spirit to unite in the great work of winning others to Jesus Christ and his kingdom.

This need to witness moved the Christians at Antioch to send Paul and Barnabas on that first missionary journey (Acts 13:1–15:35). It moved Paul to go to Macedonia, to Philippi, Thessalonica, Berea, on down to Athens and Corinth, and over to Ephesus (Acts 16:6–18:21).

Many Christians today have been set in motion by the same desire to communicate the gospel wherever they can. They have heard again and again the promise of their risen Lord: "But you shall receive power when the Holy Spirit has come upon you; and you shall be my witnesses in Jerusalem and in all Judea and Samaria and to the end of the earth" (Acts 1:8). They have heard the Lord's commands: to tarry, to go, to baptize (Matthew 28:19).

Sometimes the Holy Spirit gave people the power to witness through the formation of new local churches or societies. Sometimes this power led to the creation of schools, monasteries, hospitals, homes, and social agencies. But always the one supreme objective was to bring people together into the community of prayer and faith in the name of Jesus Christ. We should never forget that those who have worked together in our local churches and on the mission fields of the world often ran into difficulties, sometimes violent opposition. Christians were persecuted from ancient times into the modern era. The work of the Lord Jesus Christ has never been easy. Jesus did not promise an easy time for his followers, but he did promise them the sustaining and empowering presence of the Spirit. The blood of the martyrs has indeed been the seed of the church.

Augustine was keenly aware of the difficulties. He may be allowed here to represent thousands of others. He spoke of striving for souls as "a mighty load, grevious toil." And so it has always been. For this reason many in all centuries have taken refuge in the easier ways. Many also worked hard and shared in the "grevious toil." The ongoing church of Jesus Christ bears magnificent testimony to their faithfulness.

The great question for our time is Have we tarried in Jerusalem until we also have been filled with "the power from on high"? Is not this power the final basis for the renewal of the church?

CHAPTER 5

The Holy Spirit and the Wesleyan
Emphasis on Christian Experience

When we think of the Holy Spirit in relation to Christian experience, our minds naturally turn to John Wesley. He guided his followers into the particular understanding of the Holy Spirit that has always characterized the people called Methodists, when at their best. Other important leaders in the emphasis on the Holy Spirit were Francis Asbury, Jacob Albright, Philip William Otterbein, and many others who shared deeply with Wesley in his emphasis on the work of the Holy Spirit.

Wesley emphasized *vitally experienced religion*, in contrast to ceremonialism, legalism, mysticism, or intellectualism. He preached against the idea that God had preordained all things, especially who would and who would not be saved. Wesley taught the necessity of righteous living in accordance with God's commandments, in contrast to those who held that faith alone is necessary to salvation. He felt compelled to proclaim the Holy Spirit's power to transform fallen people into new creations and to set them on their way toward holy living.

In designing City Road Chapel in London, John Wesley repeatedly used the symbol of the encircled dove around the front of the entire gallery. Sermon, prayer, hymn, class meeting, and Christian living were permeated with the presence and power of the Holy Spirit. This apostolic affirmation of the life-changing, continuing activity of the Holy Spirit was a primary characteristic of the Wesleyan movement.

In his brief comments on Paul's words on the law of the Spirit and related matters, Wesley emphasized, as did Paul, the sway of the Holy Spirit over our lives. Those who walk not after the flesh but after the Spirit (Romans 8:5) are guided in thought, word, and deed by the Spirit of God. Those "in the Spirit" (8:9) are under his government. And those "led by the Spirit of God" (8:14) are in all the ways of righteousness. Wesley understood this work of the Holy Spirit within the context of the whole sweep of revealed religion. The biblical revelation of God as Creator, Redeemer, and Holy Spirit was always kept intact, with never any danger of lapsing into a unitarianism of the Spirit.

Some people so emphasize the activity of the Holy Spirit that they tend to forget about the Father and the Son. A primary error of sect-type thought is that it tends to take an aspect of Christian truth and make it either the center or the whole of it. John Wesley avoided that error. He viewed the activity of the Holy Spirit as expressing the revealed purpose of God in Christ to remake the lives of all people and to sustain them for righteous living. The Holy Spirit's work is not only with the new birth but with the whole of real religion.

On the basis of Scripture, Wesley taught that the Holy Spirit is present and active in *every major stage of Christian experience*. A religion that is not experienced is dead and fruitless. Wesley taught that the Holy Spirit's activity needs to be identified in the *stages* leading toward righteousness through faith in Jesus Christ. God is concerned with an inner transformation that leads directly into deeds of love and mercy. Let us observe here that we are dealing with Wesley's understanding of the *primary* and *indispensable* stages in the formation of the Christian life. He believed that, in unusual instances, the Holy Spirit might act to make people speak in unknown tongues or to cure diseases or to perform miracles, but never emphasized these elements as essential to our salvation.

The Holy Spirit and Prevenient Grace

Beginning on the first level or stage, Wesley believed that the Holy Spirit is present in *everyone* even before conversion. No one is without the activity of the Holy Spirit on this preliminary level. This manifestation of the Spirit was called prevenient grace—the grace or the presence of the Holy Spirit that precedes the grace that comes with the acceptance of Jesus Christ as Lord.

Wesley believed that human nature, in its unredeemed or natural state, is sinful. It is infected with a radical evil. This condition is incurable apart from divine grace. For this reason, people cannot be filled with righteous impulses unless they are redeemed and empowered by the Holy Spirit. But, if people are thus naturally inclined toward evil and that continually, how is it possible for them to turn to God at all?

John Calvin answered this question by saying that some are simply *elected* by God for salvation and others are not. Wesley answered the question by saying that the Holy Spirit is at work in all human beings to help them open their souls to God. Salvation is not for the chosen few but for everyone. Salvation is possible because the Holy Spirit is at work on this preparatory level (prevenient grace) in all human beings.

The Holy Spirit and Justification

The Holy Spirit is present also in helping us have faith in God's forgiving love in Jesus Christ. God has already done everything needed in order to forgive us. But we do not always easily accept God's wonderful, marvelous, forgiving grace through Jesus Christ crucified. The Holy Spirit helps us repent and gratefully receive God's act of wiping the slate clean. And, of course, on the basis of Scripture, Wesley held that God's justifying or forgiving grace was made available through the mighty supernatural action in Jesus Christ crucified and risen.

The Holy Spirit and the New Birth

According to Wesley, the new birth is the beginning of inner righteousness or of what he called inner holiness. At the moment we are justified—that is, forgiven—God moves into our souls and re-creates them. Paul had this in mind when he said, "Therefore, if any one is in Christ, he is a new creation; the old has passed away, behold, the new has come" (2 Corinthians 5:17). On one occasion Wesley said that God used the same kind of creative power to convert a soul or to bring about a new birth as was required to create the world. This statement suggests how seriously Wesley took the importance of being re-created by the power of the Spirit for the purpose of living the new life of righteousness.

This *re-creation* cannot be accomplished by our own strength. Because we are sinners and pull away from Christ and the things of God, we are ineffective in solving our own basic moral and spiritual problems. Wesley was very strong in his emphasis on the universality of sin and on the fact that a gravitational pull away from the kingdom and righteousness of God exists in all of us. Therefore, we require a transformation in the very substance of our being. Jesus knew this basic human weakness when he said to Nicodemus, "You must be born anew" (John 3:7).

If we were all right by nature, we would not need to be born again. If we could be made fully right with God through culture, politeness, and education, we would not need to be born anew. The Bible teaches that we require the supernatural action of God for this new birth that Jesus and Paul spoke of and that John Wesley emphasized. The Holy Spirit moves mysteriously into our souls to re-create them through the power and presence of the living Christ.

I know that some people speak rather lightly of "born-again Christians." But we should not let such speaking turn our thoughts away from the profound reality of God's mighty action remaking our souls for righteous and creative Christian living. We are born again not through our own action but by the assistance and power of the Holy Spirit who brings the presence of the risen Christ to our heart.

Wesley defined the new birth as follows:

> It is that great change which God works in the soul when he brings it into life; when he raises it from the death of sin to the life of righteousness." (*Works*, Volume VI, page 71)

If we ask what kind of specific changes are made in our souls through this marvelous action of the Holy Spirit in the new birth, we will find a number of answers. To begin with, Jesus Christ is in command of our lives. For another thing, we have a new sense of direction or purpose. We realize that God has a plan for our lives and we have become a part of that plan. Our standards and values change. Things that once seemed important have been pushed to one side and we live by a totally new system of priorities and values. We have a new feeling toward the people around us, beginning at home. Within us grows the power of a new affection, a new capacity to love others and appreciate them for what they are and what they have been. We have new policies regarding the making and spending of money. Here we have a sense of responsibility not only to our families and ourselves but also to the proper involvement of time and money in relation to the needs of other human beings.

We have inner peace and joy. I know that Christians always have struggles and problems as do others. But in and through the entire process Christ gives an inner peace and joy that the world cannot give. We form new habits. We begin to obey God's command to pray regularly and to worship faithfully. Intercessory prayer becomes a part of our daily experience. Returning to words of Scripture becomes a habit. And we have a sense of destiny because we know that we are headed for the Kingdom of heaven beyond this life.

The Witness of the Spirit

Wesley taught that every Christian has the high privilege to experience what has been known historically as "the witness of the Spirit." Paul said that the Spirit bears witness with our spirits that we are the children of God (Romans 8:15-16; Galatians 4:6-7). All of us have many moods and varying degrees of awareness of the presence of God in our hearts. Every Christian, from time to time, is entitled to the experience of knowing through the inner witness of the Holy Spirit that he or she is the child of God. This experience is simply the immediate and direct awareness of the fact that we are pardoned by God's grace and are indeed the children of God who have been re-created by God's grace.

The Holy Spirit and Sanctification

Following the new birth, the Holy Spirit moves mysteriously into our souls to enable them to grow in grace. God's purpose is that each of us move toward perfection in love toward God and toward other human beings. So, as Wesley said, the new birth is the gate to sanctification. "When we are born again, then our sanctification, our inward and outward holiness, begins; and thenceforward we are gradually to 'grow up in Him who is our Head.' " Then Wesley added, "A child is born of a woman in a moment, or at least in a very short time: Afterward he gradually and slowly grows, till he attains to the stature of a man. In like manner, a child is born of God in a short time, if not in a moment. But it is by slow degrees that he afterward grows up to the measure of the full stature of Christ" (*Works*, Volume VI, pages 74-75).

The nature of a newborn baby is to grow. So it is in the spiritual life. The doctrine of sanctification expresses the principle of spiritual growth by the power of the Holy Spirit. According to Wesley, the Bible teaches that the Holy Spirit is the only power that can *continue* what was begun in the new birth. Christian growth is not merely a human process, but a divine reality.

The Christian always faces the danger of turning away or of backsliding. The Bible warns us of this danger from beginning to end. But we know that the Holy Spirit is ever present to "keep what has been committed to him against that day." Therefore, the same faith that we needed for our justification and new birth is needed also for the ongoing Christian life. We live and breathe and grow spiritually by grace through faith. By faith we receive those many daily blessings that God graciously gives to us. Even though we grow in grace by faith, we must do our part. Our part consists of prayer, reading the Bible, sharing in the Lord's Supper, attending faithfully upon the services of public worship, listening to the Word as it is preached, and devoting ourselves to instruction from our leaders. And, as important as anything, is our putting into practice what we know we ought to do for ourselves and others. For "faith apart from works is dead" (James 2:26). In a word, we must trust and obey.

A further word concerning prayer is in order. God commands us to pray. Our deepest needs require that we pray. Intercessory prayer is indispensable to true Christian growth. When we pray for others, our wills are directed toward their concerns and needs. Intercessory prayer is one of the most profound motivating powers for righteousness and for good deeds in the whole world. So we are commanded to enter into the life of prayer and to ask God for all the things the living Christ would want us to request.

I know that Wesley also believed in sanctification as a second definite work of grace in which the whole inner soul of a human being is purified by the supernatural action of the Holy Spirit. There are Christians today who follow in the Wesleyan heritage in emphasizing this particular way of thinking of sanctification. If God acts mightily in such a second definite work of grace by which the whole inner soul is purified, refined, and empowered for mission, then we can give glory to God. Generally speaking, however, Wesley emphasized sanctification as a process of Christian growth made possible by the supernatural initiative of the Holy Spirit who causes the living Christ to reign in our hearts and who floods our souls with Christ's love.

We know from the teaching of the Bible and from experience that we have recurring tendencies to grow cold in our Christian experience. Therefore all of us need times of renewal and rededication. The Holy Spirit works in us personally and through the church to bring times of spiritual renewal. As in nearly every stage of our Christian life, the Holy Spirit moves into us both suddenly and gradually. Unless we experience some things suddenly, we are not apt to experience them at all. Unless we experience many things gradually, our Christian life is bound to be superficial.

From the Wesleyan emphasis on the Holy Spirit, we learn that the nature of the Spirit is to act purposively. The Spirit is headed somewhere and wants to take us along. Where? Toward inner holiness that leads to outer holiness. The Holy Spirit is God's grace acting, moving, stirring within us as the Will to Love. Hence, the Spirit brings the living Christ into our souls and fills us with his compassion and concern. All persons, then, who are filled with the Spirit necessarily act to do all the good possible in behalf of others. Just as Jesus looked on every human being as precious, and identified himself with "one of the least" (Matthew 25:40), so do we through the presence of the living Christ.

CHAPTER 6

Historical Movements
for Church Renewal

The Biblical Background

During the many centuries of the Hebrew-Christian heritage, God brought his people times of spiritual renewal. God saw how much they needed renewal because they often forgot their covenant, disobeyed God, and went their own ways.

These times of spiritual awakening came primarily through the prophets who called the people to renew their commitment to God. Isaiah led the way in his day when he "saw the Lord sitting upon a throne, high and lifted up; and his train filled the temple" (6:1). Isaiah knew he was in the presence of the absolutely holy God (6:3). He saw signs and wonders (6:4). And he said: "Woe is me! For I am lost; for I am a man of unclean lips, and I dwell in the midst of a people of unclean lips; for my eyes have seen the King, the LORD of hosts!" (6:5). Then God took away Isaiah's guilt and forgave his sins. And Isaiah said: "I heard the voice of the Lord saying, 'Whom shall I send, and who will go for us?' " Isaiah responded, "Here am I! Send me" (6:7-8).

In his early prophetic ministry (beginning around 742 B.C.), Isaiah confronted the people of Judah with their religious disloyalty, social injustice, and brutality, especially in the ruling classes. He pronounced doom on those in positions of power. But he went on to bring hope to the people with God's promise of new life to all who wait for the Lord (40:31). Back of Isaiah's call to spiritual renewal were two realities: his vision of the unutterable greatness and holiness of God, and his sense of the depths of human sinfulness.

Jeremiah (born around 650 B.C.) told the people that God was going to punish them for their disobedience. He was arrested and beaten for predicting the fall of Jerusalem. His prediction came true when Jerusalem fell to Babylon and the king and many people were taken captive to Babylon. Jeremiah did not see any easy or early return of the people from their captivity. But he did lift up the vision of God's coming "new covenant with the house of Israel and the house of Judah" (31:31). For the Lord said, "And they shall be my people, and I will be their God" (32:38).

To mention one more prophet, Ezekiel was a man who had many visions. He was taken captive to Babylon, along with several thousand others (around 597 B.C.). He saw this captivity as an expression of the judgment of God because the people were constantly disobedient. Among his visions was the valley of dry bones (37:1-14). The dry bones represented the people of Israel, because they were spiritually dead, lost, and without hope. So God commanded Ezekiel to prophesy to the bones. And when he did, the bones began to come together. God put sinews, flesh, and skin on the bones. They were raised from the dead and given new life. So was it to be for the whole house of Israel.

God spoke through Ezekiel saying, "And I will put my Spirit within you, and you shall live" (37:14). Here again the vision of spiritual renewal was not to take place by something within humans. Rather, it was to be by the power of the Spirit God at work in humankind.

In the New Testament, we see God at work in special ways for the spiritual awakening of people. The primary focus is on the marvelous work of God in the life, death, and resurrection of Jesus. It came to further expression in the body of Christ (the church) at Pentecost. There, in fulfillment of Joel's prophecy (2:28-32), the apostles and others were "filled with the Holy Spirit" (Acts 2:1-4).

One of the great lessons we learn from that eternal moment in the destiny of humankind is that it did not happen like a bolt out of the blue. It was prepared for through the visions of Isaiah, Jeremiah, Ezekiel, Joel, and others. It was prepared for by the faithfulness of Jesus Christ to his unique mission as the Son of God, the Savior, and the Inaugurator of the new era of God's kingdom. It was prepared for by the experiences of the apostles as they walked and worked with Jesus. Then and only then could the sudden empowering "from on high" (Luke 24:49) occur.

Not by accident have all genuine Christian efforts for spiritual awakening and renewal gone back to the biblical models, particularly to Pentecost and the directives of apostolic Christianity. What were the essential elements of Pentecost and apostolic Christianity? We may list at least seven elements of paramount significance: (1) the centrality of Jesus Christ, crucified and risen; (2) the supernatural initiative and power of the Holy Spirit; (3) the transformation and absolute commitment of people to Jesus Christ and his kingdom through the indwelling presence of the Holy Spirit; (4) powerful preaching of the gospel and effective teaching on the kingdom of God and righteousness; (5) specific manifestations of the power of the Holy Spirit and continuing blessings through the Holy Spirit; (6) the formation of people into the community of prayer, faith, and work (the body of Christ); and (7) world evangelization.

These would seem to be the essential elements in that first Christian Pentecost and in the apostolic Christianity that followed it. We may doubt that a sustained renewal of the church will ever happen apart from these divinely appointed realities.

Some Early Warnings and Guidelines

Even the apostles had instructions concerning the dangers of emphasizing "signs and wonders" (Acts 14:3) apart from the larger context of the love of Christ. Paul instructed the Christians at Corinth on both the importance and dangers of the gifts or manifestations of the Spirit (see 1 Corinthians 12–14). He pointed out that the primary mission of the Holy Spirit is to enable us truly to proclaim that "Jesus is Lord" (1 Corinthians 12:3). The varieties of gifts of the Spirit are to unite us as Christians—never to make us divisive. "To each is given the manifestation of the Spirit for the common good" (verse 7).

It is interesting to observe that in 1 Corinthians 12:7-11, Paul spoke of the *manifestation* of the Spirit in various ways. The specific exception has to do with the *gifts* of healing. Regarding all these manifestations of the Spirit within the "body of Christ" (verse 27), Paul suggested that not all persons are to have the same gifts or manifestations. "Are all apostles? Are all prophets? Are all teachers? Do all work miracles? Do all possess gifts of healing? Do all speak with tongues? Do all interpret? But earnestly desire the higher gifts" (verses 29-31).

Paul made special mention of speaking in tongues. Evidently the practice was causing problems in the church at Corinth (14:2-4). Then he went on and said in some detail: "So with yourselves; since you are eager for manifestations of the Spirit, strive to excel in building up the church" (verse 12). This passage suggests that one of the surest manifestations of the Spirit is that of building up the church. Paul added: "I thank God that I speak in tongues more than you all; nevertheless, in church I would rather speak five words with my mind, in order to instruct others, than ten thousand words in a tongue" (verses 18-19). Obviously, Paul was referring to what goes on *in church,* where the community of prayer and faith is gathered. In commending the "more excellent way," he moved into his great chapter on love (Chapter 13).

Soon after the days of the apostles the need for some kind of guidelines regarding the special gifts of the Spirit arose. The church at its best has always been a Spirit-filled and hence a Spirit-motivated movement. But it has had to deal with the recurring tensions between orderliness and vitality, structure and dynamics. A second-century document, the *Didache* (did'-ih-key), dealt with this problem. It was written by a church administrator who concluded that the only way to preserve the Spirit's power within the church was to provide guidelines. Spiritual gifts in general, and prophecy in particular, could be counterfeited. Jesus himself had warned against false prophets (Matthew 7:15), even when they showed "signs and wonders" (24:24). And we know that even in the early days "many false prophets [had] gone out into the world" (1 John 4:1-3).

Much of the *Didache* was devoted to instructions on how to test the authenticity of gifts of the Spirit. The major responsibility for such testing was given to deacons and bishops. Jesus had stated the great test: "You will know them by their fruits" (Matthew 7:16). And John had put it this way: "By this you know the Spirit of God: every spirit which confesses that Jesus Christ has come in the flesh is of God, and every spirit which does not confess Jesus is not of God" (1 John 4:2-3). Other guidelines were furnished by the ancient creeds. But these concerned matters of doctrine rather than the gifts of the Spirit.

Some Representative Examples of Renewal Movements

Some persons suppose that after the days of the apostles very little emphasis was placed on the special manifestations or gifts of the Spirit. But this is doubtful. For example, Irenaeus (130?–200), who was a great Christian theologian and defender of the faith, said that speaking in tongues (glossolalia) was commonly practiced in various churches. He observed that though he himself did not speak in tongues, many others did. E. Glenn Hinson, basing his conclusion on important studies of Heinrich Weinel (1899) and others, says: "In the second and early third centuries . . . the evidences for glossolalia . . . apart from Montanism are substantial."

We may refer to Montanism as an example of an early charismatic movement that had wide influence. It began around the middle of the second century. It got its name from its founder, Montanus. We know very little about him.

The early church historian Eusebius (260?–340?) said of him that at times he would be overcome by sudden seizures, fall into trances, and speak in unknown tongues. Montanus is said to have had his first such experience around A.D. 156. His followers believed that the Holy Spirit gave him special revelations. He and two notable women, Prisca and Maximilla, presented themselves as prophets. Mass conversions took place. The movement spread as far as North Africa and Rome and was given considerable impetus when Tertullian of Carthage (160?–230?) became a Montanist and the movement's most famous convert around A.D. 200. Tertullian was one of the most learned and respected church fathers.

Montanists were opposed from the start by many church leaders. This opposition was not based on their emphasis on the presence and power of the Holy Spirit. Nor was it based on their speaking in tongues. Rather, it was based on two things. First, the Montanists were opposed because they believed that the Holy Spirit carried Christians beyond the Old Testament and Pentecost into a new dispensation. The Montanists claimed that the Holy Spirit spoke in *new* revelations through the ecstatic experiences and "prophecies" of Montanus. They believed that Christians were to become passive organs of the Spirit who was manifested through special gifts, especially through visions and prophecies. They proclaimed the "new age of the Spirit" and the imminent return of Christ. They wanted to revive the sense of *immediacy* in the church because, they felt, the church had lost the sense of expectancy. They did not want to separate from the church. They wanted to reform it. They accepted the major doctrines of the church, but their emphasis on gifts of the Spirit, especially prophecy, became a problem.

Second, the Montanists were opposed because of the rigorous rules of conduct that, they insisted, should be accepted by *all* Christians. They were alarmed over the complacency within the church. They declared that their rigorous practices alone were the true expressions of biblical holiness. They insisted on regular days of prayer and fasting. They opposed second marriages. Women were to wear veils. Second repentance was denied. And any who fell away were refused readmission. The fact is that many people were drawn to Montanism by its appeal to self-denial and by its sense of the immediate and specific actions of the Holy Spirit.

After many years of rumors, lies, denunciations, discussions, and debates, Montanism was officially repudiated by the church in the fourth century.

God calls us to learn from history. As Robert Tuttle has said regarding Montanism: "This is a classic example of a Spirit movement that outlived its time. Its sectarian nature did not drop away after its point was made." He adds, "Again, the effectiveness of any movement of the Spirit depends on its ability to join hands with the main body once its point has been made or the main body has responded appropriately" (*Wind and Flame* [Graded Press, 1978]; pages 46-47).

In the twelfth century, Joachim Fiore, seeing the desperate plight of the church, predicted the imminent coming of the Age of the Spirit. The declining church would be revived by the Holy Spirit and the gospel would be carried throughout the world.

The movement led by Francis of Assisi (1182–1226), with its emphasis on poverty and elemental deeds of love, was Spirit-filled. It carried on its mission within the main body of the church. As it developed, however, it deviated often from its original significance as a movement of the Spirit.

In England, John Wycliffe (1324–1384) was affirming the supreme authority of the Bible and leading in the task of translating it into the English language. On the Continent many forces were at work preparing the way for Luther and the Reformation. Luther, Calvin, and others emphasized the work of the Holy Spirit in illuminating the Bible and bringing the Word of God home to people. At the same time, there was a lack of adequate emphasis on how the Holy Spirit works, *specifically* and *directly*, within the souls of people. Nevertheless, the Reformation was a Spirit-filled movement. Only the presence of the Holy Spirit would be adequate to recover that grand biblical theme of justification by grace through faith. Good works were said to flow from the Holy Spirit.

Under the influence of George Fox (1624–1691) and others, the Quakers emphasized both the inner spiritual life and the outer demands for economic justice. They opposed slavery and championed the causes of the poor. Fox often felt himself to be illuminated both by the Bible and by the Holy Spirit. His efforts at social reform may be seen as a direct outcome of the presence of the Holy Spirit in his life.

An example of another kind of movement of the Spirit took place under the leadership of Count N. L. von Zinzendorf. After graduating from the university at Halle, he established in 1724 a community of Christian refugees on his estate. He named it *Herrnhut*, meaning "The Lord's watch" (see Isaiah 62:1, 6-7). Among those present in this community were Moravians, Reformed, and Catholics. Zinzendorf had difficulty organizing them into a united body. But after four years of quarreling among factions, in August 1727 the community experienced a baptism of the Holy Spirit at a communion service. They became a united community of round-the-clock prayer for the whole church as well as for one another.

Around the same time in America what has been called the Great Awakening took place. It will be remembered that George Whitefield (1714–1770)—who influenced Wesley to preach in the open air—came to America and preached in many places. His preaching and that of Jonathan Edwards (1703–1758) combined with that of others to bring about the Great Awakening.

The Wesleyan Revival

We need to consider now in more detail one of the most remarkable movements of the Holy Spirit for renewal in the church. It took place under the leadership of John Wesley (1703–1791) and has been called the eighteenth-century evangelical revival. We have already seen in Chapter 5 that Wesley emphasized the work of the Holy Spirit in every stage of the Christian life. Love is at the heart of that life. And that love is born in us by the grace of God through the Holy Spirit.

In his sermon on "The Witness of Our Own Spirit,"

Wesley said, "By 'the grace of God' is sometimes to be understood that free love, that unmerited mercy, by which I a sinner, through the merits of Christ, am now reconciled to God. But in this place [2 Corinthians 1:12] it rather means that power of God the Holy Ghost which 'worketh in us both to will and to do of his good pleasure' " (Philippians 2:13) [*The Works of John Wesley*, Volume 1 (Abingdon Press, 1984); page 309]. It is clear that Wesley's view was that God's grace is the work of the Holy Spirit within us. Again and again Wesley emphasized the theme that the Holy Spirit is the life of God within the human soul. That life is the Will to Love.

Wesley knew that people are sinners who, even after conversion, are in constant danger of turning away from their Lord. Therefore, the new life in Christ is possible only by the supernatural inflowing of the Holy Spirit. In this way alone are we born into love, grow in love, and moved toward perfection in love.

John Wesley traveled around 250,000 miles—most of it on horseback—and preached over 40,000 sermons. Charles Wesley preached many sermons and wrote thousands of hymns and thus made many significant contributions to the eighteenth-century evangelical revival. But none of these impressive facts explains fully the spiritual awakening that took place in England. What were the major factors at work under the inspiration of the Holy Spirit? I suggest at least six factors.

1. The strong and balanced emphasis on the authority and finality of the Bible as God's living Word was accepted as the only final guide in doctrine and in practice. Of course, Wesley knew that the Bible had to be interpreted and that equally dedicated Christians might be led to different interpretations of certain passages. One of the most important aids to interpreting the Bible is our Christian *experience*; that is, what we find confirmed in the ongoing of our lives as Christians.

And, of course, Wesley believed that *tradition* and *reason* are aids to understanding the Bible. He knew well that we ignore to our peril the great heritage of Christianity. In addition, he appealed to people to use their God-given reason in interpreting Scripture. It is a matter of special interest that John Milton, in his *Paradise Lost*, portrayed Satan as opposed both to love and to reason. For, as Milton said, love "hath his seat in Reason" and at the same time "refines the thoughts" (Book 8, lines 589, 91).

2. The Holy Spirit moved into the hearts of people to enable them to make a personal commitment to Jesus Christ. The Savior was not merely a distant figure but an experienced presence. In other words, a very important factor in the Wesleyan evangelical revival was the emphasis on *experienced* religion. God promised this Christianity "as an inward principle," and everyone needed it. Wesley said, "And this I conceive to be the strongest evidence of the truth of Christianity" (*Letters*, Volume II [Epworth Press, 1931]; page 383).

3. The Holy Spirit worked through the disciplined living of the people called Methodists. Wesley knew as well as anyone that no vital Christianity can exist without discipline. In his earlier days, he tended toward a rigorous legalism. But after his heartwarming experience, he emphasized as the motivating principle the grace of God—the Holy Spirit within. Prayer, Bible study, good reading, participation in the societies and in the small groups (of from six to ten persons) known as bands, sharing of burdens, intercession, regular attendance upon the Sacrament of the Lord's Supper, and unhesitating service to others in need—all of these were elements in the disciplined living of the Methodists. To what end? To inward and outward holiness; that is, to the inner dynamic of love and the outward expression of it in good deeds. Wesley said that the portrait of a Christian is given in the Sermon on the Mount (Matthew 5–7) and in 1 Corinthians 13. "Christianity promises this character shall be mine, if I will not rest till I attain it" (*Letters*, Volume II, page 381).

The genius of Wesley was at no point more evident than in his ability to organize his followers into societies and bands that accepted disciplined living. In this he built upon the apostles and anticipated much that is said today on church growth. He saw that for most people discipline must go beyond self-discipline into group-discipline. Therefore,

Wesley personally took responsibility for discipline within the societies. They were his primary centers for teaching Methodist doctrine. The Holy Spirit used those organized groups as a wonderful means for awakening, nurturing, and motivating the people. There the new converts gathered after conversion (justification and the new birth). There they were taught that they must continue in the Christian way by the inner working of the Holy Spirit toward perfection in love.

4. Another factor in the Wesleyan revival—often overlooked or minimized—was the preaching and singing. Wesley and his preachers proclaimed the gospel. Wesley guided their thinking so they understood the great doctrines of justification by faith and the new birth. He and his preachers taught them, preached them, and sang about them. They expressed their experience of joy and praise as they shared together in song.

5. The Holy Spirit moved the people called Methodists not only to feel but to *do*. They were impelled by the Holy Spirit to help people who were in need. The Holy Spirit used community service as a means for bringing about the Wesleyan evangelical revival.

6. The Holy Spirit inspired the Methodists with the lively hope of heaven. The biblical teaching on God's great plan of eternal life for his children delivers people from despair, moves them to rejoice in the presence of their risen Lord, and stirs them up to good works. As Charles Wesley wrote:

> To him our willing hearts we give
> Who gives us power and peace,
> And dead to sin, his members live
> The life of righteousness;
> The hidden life of Christ is ours
> With Christ concealed above,
> And tasting the celestial powers,
> We banquet on his love.
>
> (*The Book of Hymns*, Number 457)

CHAPTER 7

The Contemporary
Charismatic Movement

We have heard that the contemporary charismatic movement is the most important sign of renewal in the church throughout the world today. That remains to be seen. But this much is sure: Millions of Christians throughout the world, including those in the mainline churches, are feeling the influence of the charismatic movement.

In this chapter I shall present the following information: (1) definitions of the terms *charismatic* and *charismatic movement*; (2) a brief historical statement; (3) a summary of the major emphases of the charismatic movement; (4) some problems; and (5) a comparison of the contemporary charismatic movement with the Wesleyan emphasis on the Holy Spirit.

Definitions

The word *charismatic* comes from the Greek word *charisma*, meaning gift. The term *charismatic movement* refers then to those groups of Christians who emphasize certain special gifts or manifestations of the Holy Spirit in addition to the gift of salvation. These gifts or manifestations are the ones referred to by Paul in 1 Corinthians 12:4-11. In broader scope, they include other lists in Paul's writings (see Romans 12:6-8; Ephesians 4:11-13).

A Brief Historical Statement

Various charismatic movements have taken place throughout Christian history. But except for the movement known as Montanism—which was discussed in the preceding chapter—relatively little was reported about them. For example, after A.D. 250 the gift of speaking in tongues was seldom mentioned in the writings of the church leaders. By the fourth century it was virtually unknown to Chrysostom (345?–407) in the Greek community and to Augustine (354–430) in the Latin community. Both of them tended to assume that the gift of tongues—to mention one particular gift—was a special sign in the earliest days of Christianity but was no longer useful.

Even the writers of the Middle Ages left little in the way of evidence of Christians speaking in tongues. Since then, scattered groups in the seventeenth and eighteenth centuries, including the Jansenists (a Catholic holiness order), Quakers, Shakers, and others, claimed the gift of tongues. But they did not make it a central feature of their experience. I mention speaking in tongues not because that is at the heart of the contemporary charismatic movement but as an illustration only.

We should notice—as John Wesley said—that the silence of writers on the special gifts of the Holy Spirit does not mean that the gifts were absent. After all, many experiences of the presence and power of the Holy Spirit have gone unreported, today as well as in the past. Think of the millions of Christians in Latin America, Africa, Asia, Europe, and North America today who experience unusual outpourings of the Holy Spirit. How many of their experiences and testimonies are actually reported in writing?

Historically, from time to time many groups of Christians have claimed that the Holy Spirit was at work in their lives in undeniable ways. The Wesleyan revival was undoubtedly a movement of the Spirit among the masses of England. Its primary focus was on the power of the Spirit to transform the lives of people and to set them on the way to right living. The action of the Holy Spirit was felt not only in individuals but in individuals in small groups of people who shared in the desire to flee "from the wrath to come" (1 Thessalonians 1:10) and to be made right with God and with other human beings. In a word, the aim of the Wesleyan revival was to experience and spread scriptural holiness.

In the United States one kind of holiness movement with a Wesleyan emphasis on the Holy Spirit stressed sanctification as a second definite work of grace. The basic idea was that Jesus Christ had far more to offer than a new beginning (forgiveness and the new birth). That "more" was the continuing presence of the Holy Spirit purifying the soul and making it holy.

For example, Charles G. Finney, a Presbyterian who was influenced by Wesley's teaching on holiness, preached and taught that every Christian should expect and experience the ongoing power of the Spirit. He was born in America in 1792, a year after Wesley died, and was the first to popularize the term *baptism of the Spirit*. He was one of the foremost leaders in the holiness movement that stressed sanctification as a second definite work of grace. At the same time, Finney was aware of the inadequacies of the enthusiasm of the camp meetings when not accompanied by sound theology, social concern, and involvement in the local church. One of his most important concerns was the practice of prayer. He was a leader in the prayer movements of his day.

On one side was the holiness movement—with Wesleyan emphases—stressing the definite power of the Holy Spirit who makes for holiness by faith. Here the emphasis was on sanctification as a second definite work of grace without significant interest in other special gifts of the Holy Spirit, such as speaking in tongues.

On another side was the pentecostal movement, which owed little to the Wesleyan heritage. It began in the United States in 1900. The pentecostal groups began by stressing "baptism in the spirit" with a strong emphasis on speaking in tongues as a necessary sign of the baptism. They showed also an openness to such other gifts of the Spirit as healing, prophecy, and the exorcism of evil spirits.

From the start these early pentecostal groups tended to be hostile to higher education and theological education for ministers. They believed the Holy Spirit would inspire the ministers and other leaders on what to say and guide them on what to do. In addition, there was the practice of spiritual healing without the benefit of medical doctors. Pentecostals believed that reliance on medical resources was a sure sign of lack of faith. They considered academic studies unnecessary. Indeed, they believed such study interfered with the free movement of the Spirit. These beliefs separated the pentecostal churches from the mainline churches where institutions of higher learning and medicine were prominent features of their service in the world. Another divisive factor was the insistence on speaking in tongues *as a necessary sign of baptism in the Spirit.*

Nevertheless, today the pentecostal movement, despite its many diverse and even independent churches, is a major force within contemporary Christendom. The estimate is that between two and three million Christians in the United States are members of pentecostal churches where speaking in tongues is practiced. Because of its missionary outreach, the pentecostal movement here has become a part of the worldwide charismatic reality. The largest Protestant local church in the world is a Korean charismatic church with over 200,000 members.

The charismatic movement, which emphasizes special gifts of the Holy Spirit, has become visible more recently in the form of neopentecostalism (pentecostalism within the Roman Catholic and Protestant churches). It differs from earlier pentecostal movements in a number of ways. It favors higher education and an educated ministry. It favors both prayer and medicine as combining God's total healing delivery system. It seeks to avoid divisiveness by emphasizing the centrality of Christ, the ultimacy of Christian love, and the importance of the ecumenical spirit. These differences mean, among other things, that in the contemporary charismatic movement, persons who experience certain special gifts of the Spirit do not consider themselves superior to those who experience the universal gifts of the Spirit—faith, hope, and love. Nor do they consider any *special gift* of the Spirit as essential to salvation.

At the local level this charismatic movement emphasizes "baptism in the Spirit," followed by such special gifts or manifestations of the Spirit as speaking in tongues, healing, discernment, and so on. Special emphasis is put on the gift of healing, which is given both to those who are God's agents of healing and to the healed. Other gifts in keeping with 1 Corinthians 12:4-11 are also recognized. An important feature of neopentecostalism is the emphasis on the centrality of Christ and the primary Christian virtues—faith, hope, and love. Prayers of intercession and praise are inherent features of the contemporary charismatic reality. The movement is marked also by the passion for worldwide evangelization.

Within the mainline churches the contemporary charismatic movement—with several million adherents—functions in small groups of people who meet for Bible study, intercessory prayer, and services of praise and healing. These persons are faithful in attending and supporting, with their prayers, action, and gifts, the programs of their local churches. Occasionally, many mainline churches hold services of healing that are frequently planned in keeping with the traditions of the particular denominations. For example, many healing services include the Sacrament of Holy Communion as well as appropriate sermons, hymns of praise and rededication, prayers, and the laying on of hands. The movement encourages commitment to the local churches as ordained of God. From time to time contemporary charismatic Christians come together for large regional, national, and international conferences. At these conferences, they sing songs of praise, hear prominent lecturers, engage in Bible study, share in prayers of intercession, and participate in healing services.

One of the largest charismatic communities in the United States is an ecumenical group called the Word of God Community. It is the world headquarters of the Catholic Charismatic Renewal and is based in Ann Arbor, Michigan.

A Summary of Major Emphases of the Charismatic Movement

At the theological level, contemporary charismatic groups devote considerable attention to classifying and interpreting the kinds of gifts of the Spirit referred to by Paul. These gifts include vocal gifts (prophecy, speaking in tongues, and interpreting tongues); knowing gifts (discernment of spirits and of needs, knowledge, wisdom); power gifts (faith, miracles, healing); ministry gifts (apostles, evangels, pastor-teachers); administrative gifts; and gifts for building up the body of Christ. (On all of these see Romans 12:6-8; 1 Corinthians 12:4-11; 14:1-5, 9-12; 26; Ephesians 4:4-13.) The idea on which all with theological depth agree is that the varieties of gifts of the Spirit are for the building up of the body of Christ and for empowerment for world evangelization. Of course, with Paul all Christians are to desire earnestly "the higher gifts" (1 Corinthians 12:31; 13).

What are the major characteristics of the contemporary charismatic movement? This question is not easy to answer because the movement contains many movements. Against the background of what has already been said, the charismatic movements that I have in mind would hold the following understandings: (a) All Christian groups urgently need the renewing power of the Holy Spirit; (b) that power is available *now* in specific ways, and miracles are to be expected; (c) those miracles or special manifestations of the Holy Spirit are for the blessing of people, for the building up of the church, and for empowerment for mission; (d) more specifically, some of these important gifts are speaking in tongues and interpreting tongues; healing of body, mind, and spirit; teaching and preaching with prophetic power; guidance in daily living; and assistance of the Holy Spirit in all of our human concerns, including financial needs and family concerns; and (e) making wide use of radio, television, and printed materials by the charismatic movement in the United States and Canada. In all of these examples, every participant is expected to do his or her part by faith and obedience to God.

These special gifts or manifestations of the Spirit are understood to be over and above the supreme gift of salvation. And these gifts are *in* Jesus Christ, *through* Jesus Christ, and *for* Jesus Christ and his kingdom.

I may conclude this section by saying that there is no charismatic theology. There is only biblical theology with an emphasis on the specific gifts or manifestations of the Holy Spirit in the here and now.

In my judgment there are two important contributions of the charismatic movement to the Christian world today: The first is the sustained conviction that when we do our part the Holy Spirit is dynamically at work *in specific ways now,* within the community of prayer and faith, to help and bless people in every major area of their needs: spiritual, physical, emotional, intellectual, interpersonal, economical, and financial. The second is that the Holy Spirit works in all who obey God's call, to empower them *now in specific ways* for mission and world evangelization. And both contributions confirm in experience the Spirit's marvelous work and the eagerness to give glory to the Lord Jesus Christ.

Some Major Problems

We consider now three major problems.

First, despite all efforts for love and understanding, we always have the problem of divisiveness. This results in part from the attitudes of many noncharismatics who maintain what I would call strong prejudices against the claims of those who have experienced certain special gifts or manifestations of the Holy Spirit. Consequently, many charismatic Christians are made to feel ill at ease or even rejected in the churches they love. So, many deeply dedicated Christians who have much to contribute feel frustrated in the mainline churches. For the most part, however, this situation has not led them to withdraw.

On the other hand, this divisiveness results from the attitude of superiority that some charismatic Christians express in various ways. Sometimes they insist on changing the forms of worship in the mainline local churches of which they are members. They want more informality and openness to the movement of the Spirit in the regular worship services. Many would want these services to become occasions for uplifted arms in praise to God, for speaking in tongues, and for healing. Problems arise in the mainline churches when these are practiced in opposition to the majority of the members.

The problem here roots primarily in the demand on the part of many charismatic Christians that *all* who are truly filled with the Holy Spirit will necessarily receive special gifts of the Holy Spirit, such as speaking in tongues, experiences of healing, financial blessings, and so forth.

A second problem relates to the interpretation of the biblical teaching. Paul makes it clear that those who are filled with the Holy Spirit *may* receive special gifts of the Spirit, including speaking in tongues. But the heart of the biblical teaching is that the primary mission of the Holy Spirit is to magnify Jesus Christ as Lord. Everyone who is filled with the Spirit of the living Christ is in fact filled with the Holy Spirit. All such persons will express the love of Christ that Jesus summarized in the Sermon on the Mount and that Paul expressed in 1 Corinthians 13.

We can understand how anyone who receives a special gift of the Spirit might suppose that what he or she has felt should be experienced by all Christians. But this is contrary to Scripture. In addition, it is contrary to the experience of many Christians. Relatively few are given the gift of tongues. Not all are healed. Not all are delivered from desperate financial need. Not all are freed from the bondage of broken interpersonal relations. At the same time, all of us who claim the name of Jesus Christ should be grateful for the miracles received and the blessings claimed. For surely everything that truly brings deliverance in the name of the One who came to set at liberty those in captivity is of God.

I mention one more problem. Some charismatic Christians are in danger of missing God's call to churchmanship. God's administrative plan is to carry forward the work of Jesus Christ through the community of prayer and faith that bears his name. Jesus made this clear in his command to "go therefore and make disciples of all nations, baptizing them in the name of the Father and of the Son and of the Holy Spirit" (Matthew 28:19). Baptism is the sacrament of incorporation into the body of Christ—the church. The Holy Spirit expressed this by binding the earliest Christians together at Pentecost. Paul understood his mission—under the inspiration of the Holy Spirit—to preach the gospel, to teach, and to form people into the body of Christ.

Somewhere in here lies the explanation of the many charismatic denominations and independent charismatic churches on the scene in the contemporary Christian world. Surely a deeper sense of the Holy Spirit's call to unity on all sides would have led to that largeness of Christian understanding that Paul expressed so well. After referring to the various gifts or manifestations of the Spirit, Paul said: "All these are inspired by the same Spirit, who apportions to each one individually as he wills. . . . For by one spirit we were all baptized into one body . . . and all were made to drink of one Spirit" (1 Corinthians 12:11, 13). And "we, though many, are one body in Christ, and individually members one of another" (Romans 12:5).

Wesley and the Contemporary Charismatic Movement

Wesley was always open to manifestations of the Spirit. He believed in the continuing presence and activity of the Spirit. He insisted that the twofold test of the validity of any Christian experience is Scripture and the practical results. He commented with approval on certain unusual manifestations of the Spirit in his day. I believe he would do the same were he living two hundred years later.

Wesley would join most charismatic Christians who consider the Bible the only final basis for Christian belief and practice. Once more, Wesley would rejoice with nearly all Christians—Protestants, Independents, and Catholics alike—who believe that the Holy Spirit continues to perform within us after conversion, baptism, and confirmation.

Wesley recognized the reality of special gifts of the Holy Spirit even though he did not claim to have received any of them. According to him the special operations of the Spirit, following repentance, justification, and the new birth, were available to *all* Christians. Those movements of the Spirit were aimed to produce the inner witness and inward holiness. By means of the inner witness, the Spirit bears witness with our spirits that we have passed from death to life and are now truly the children of God. In addition, the Spirit fills Christians with the love of Christ and moves them *now* toward what Wesley called Christian perfection. Wesley considered his emphasis on Christian perfection to be a part of the larger heritage of the Christian religion. He felt in experience and proclaimed in his preaching the sovereign grace of the Holy Spirit whereby we have the Will to Love. The Spirit's sovereign grace and the Will to Love are inevitably expressed in action.

The contemporary charismatic movement differs from Wesley's teaching in emphasizing special gifts of the Spirit without focusing them primarily on holiness. The special gifts or manifestations are for inner joy in the Lord, for physical and emotional healing, for financial and other blessings. I am not saying that contemporary charismatic Christians are not interested in right living and holiness. They are. But for Wesley the focus of his belief in the sovereign presence and power of the Holy Spirit was on that holiness of life to which every Christian is called. Wesley's great passion was for inward and outward holiness. All Christians were to strive for this state with the confident expectation that what they could never accomplish in their own power alone would be given them by the grace of God—that is, by the supernatural infilling of the Holy Spirit. For this is a direct expression of the sovereign initiative and grace of God.

We see in Wesley's churchmanship another point of contrast. Though his bands (small groups) and societies started out as sect-type formations, he always wanted them to be closely tied to the sacraments and orders of the church. Wesley conceived his mission to include the renewal of the church through the power of the Spirit.

Wesley would have rejoiced in many manifestations of the power of the Spirit in the contemporary charismatic movement. He would have called on all Christians to move toward the inward and outward holiness that comes through disciplined and obedient openness to the Spirit. It was no accident that one of his major themes was expressed in the words of Scripture: "Strive for peace with all men, and for the holiness without which no one will see the Lord" (Hebrews 12:14).

CHAPTER 8

The Holy Spirit and Social Responsibility

Some persons suppose that the Spirit's concern is to give us inner joy and peace and to prepare us for heaven. Others suppose that the primary function of God's grace is to affect our ethical conduct so that we become social reformers. In nearly every generation of Christians battles have occurred between those who emphasized personal salvation and those who stressed the ministry to the poor, the sick, and the needy. For example, Charles G. Finney and Phoebe Palmer (a Methodist woman who was a leader in the New York revivals from 1857) believed that social reforms would automatically follow the conversion of individuals.

A historical case in point was the issue of slavery. Despite the efforts at moderation within Methodism—efforts by Bishops Asbury, McKendree, and others—this issue eventually divided the church. But Wesley himself was clear on the subject and fought against slavery as one of the most cruel of all institutions. This is another example of how Wesley's emphasis on inward and outward holiness actually functioned. As far as I know, any major area of human need of which Wesley was aware awakened a response from him. Ignorance, poverty, disease, loneliness, the prison system, drunkenness, slavery, war—these and other concerns were on his heart.

Why do we urge that the Holy Spirit is directly related to

social reforms? Because the Bible teaches that God is dynamic. God wants his goals realized. Those goals concern the well-being of people. The Holy Spirit does not act with aimless energy. The Spirit acts to bless people, to help them experience what Jesus promised, namely, that they might have life and have it more abundantly (John 10:10). The Holy Spirit acts to bring wholeness of body, mind, and spirit. The Holy Spirit yearns for all human beings on earth to enjoy that dignity and those basic rights without which people can be neither free nor happy.

The problem is that human bondage is caused not only by what individuals bring on themselves through bad habits and wrong living. Human bondage is brought on also by *social* evils. That is, human bondage comes from social structures that need to be transformed, changed for the glory of God and the blessing of people.

Two Basic Errors

I see two basic errors made regarding the presence and power of the Holy Spirit.

One error is the idea that the Holy Spirit affects the inner life and is not much concerned with deeds that affect the larger forces of history. The other error is that the Holy Spirit is actually nothing more or less than the passion for social reform. The former leads to inner joy and peace, to private devotions, and uncomplaining acceptance of one's lot in life. The latter leads to actions of the sort performed by social agencies without much interest in the dynamic presence of the Holy Spirit who motivates Christians both to win people to Jesus Christ and to champion the causes of justice and liberty.

The issue here becomes clear in the contemporary world when we reflect on war and peace. The ravages of war in Lebanon (to mention only one location) and of sporadic terrorist activity—so graphically portrayed on TV—make it clear that the Holy Spirit and war are on opposite sides. We know, of course, that when people are attacked from without or from within they are going to fight back. Therefore, when the Holy Spirit is present within us—that is, when Jesus Christ actually reigns—we have to do what we can to avoid the occasions of war. What good does it do us to talk about health of body and spirit, of the abundant life, of home and family, when bombs and bullets are killing and crippling people and destroying their hard-earned property?

On the other hand, what the advocates of social reform tend to miss is what is most important, namely, winning people to Jesus Christ and nurturing them in the faith. In the interest of liberation they often neglect the preaching of the gospel that leads to salvation. Many individuals who champion the causes of justice, peace, and humanity have not bothered to find out either how to win people to Jesus Christ or how to nurture them in Christian living.

The Most Important Thing

What is the most important thing that can happen to people? It is to enter into the life-giving relation with God through Jesus Christ. This relationship enables them to experience the joy of returning to the God who created them, and the privilege of serving in God's kingdom. This experience is enriched immeasurably when those who are thus found of God are united with others in the body of Christ. Then prayer and praise—in the homes and outside—take on new meaning. Indeed, only in this way is the sustained experience of the meaning, dignity, and destiny of life accomplished.

Though the hungry are fed, the naked clothed, and the sick given medical care, these deeds, however helpful, are wholly inadequate unless people are also introduced to Christ and united in the fellowship of prayer and faith. Why? Because without this fellowship we have deprived people of the greatest of all blessings: the life-giving faith relationship with God. World evangelization is the top priority. It is the supreme task to which Jesus called his disciples; and it is the supreme summons for our time.

Therefore, action in behalf of others is not confined to ministering to physical needs. To think in that way is to insult human beings by assuming that they are no more than physical entities. Striving for the souls of people is social action. A part of our aim in ministering to their physical needs is to enable them to open their lives to the glory of God in Jesus Christ. In the long run, a community is most enriched and blessed when the people are formed into continuing churches, schools, and hospitals where the benefits of Christ can be experienced from generation to generation.

The Tradition of Passivity

Traditions may be good or bad or a mixture of both. A tradition within Christianity that has had tragic effects is what I call the tradition of passivity. By this I mean the belief, handed down from generation to generation, that we *cannot*, or *need not*, or *should not* do anything about the larger affairs of community life.

What are these larger affairs? I mean by them the cultural, political, economic, institutional, and moral forces that affect large numbers of people in a community, nation, or world.

Those who say we *cannot* do anything about them are either fatalists or predestinarians. In either case, they tell us, the large issues such as those of war and peace, pollution, and human rights are beyond our control. So they say we can do nothing about them.

Those who say we *need not* do anything about them assume that otherwise we would be tampering with God's affairs. As a consequence, from a false sense of piety, they are deaf to the Spirit's call to responsible living in community.

This tradition of passivity has had its tragic consequences. Even the Bible has been interpreted to say, "Hands off." I once heard an internationally famous New Testament scholar say to let the church be the church on the larger social issues. In that context he insisted that we stay out of public affairs and stick to the business of prayer and worship. Of course, nothing is more important than winning people to Jesus Christ. But are Christians to have no voice in the struggles for justice and human dignity?

Even Augustine, in his *City of God,* said, in effect, that the rise and fall of empires is in the hands of God. So are the issues of war and peace.

Many Christians believe that the end of the world is near. Therefore, we need not and should not bother about what happens in the here and now. Why worry about nuclear destruction, pollution, overpopulation, or racism when the Lord is going to return soon? Along this same line, many Christians even go so far as to say that the world scene must get worse and worse before the end comes. Therefore, why bother?

I recognize that the Bible clearly teaches the end of this present temporal order. But it does not say when. Jesus mentioned certain signs (see, for example, Mark 13). But Jesus also said that even he did not know when the end would come (13:32). The basic biblical theme is this: In God's own good time and way this present order will be brought to an end and God's "new heavens and a new earth" (2 Peter 3:13) will be formed under the sovereign lordship of Jesus Christ.

When? We do not know. We know only that it is not in keeping with God's nature to make a magnificent beginning of things at creation, to marvelously provide Jesus Christ for our redemption, and then to let it all fizzle out in the end. We believe the end must be commensurate with the beginning. Therefore, we believe not merely in the end but in consummation. In God's own good time and way, Jesus Christ will return in all his glory and reign over all. His name is above every name. But when will these events occur? We do not know, for God has not revealed it. Our part is to be ready and to do God's work as long as we are here.

Jesus warned that on these matters "false Christs and false prophets will arise and show signs and wonders, to lead astray, if possible, the elect." Jesus added, "But take heed; I have told you all things beforehand" (Mark 13:22-23).

Nothing here should make us stand still. God still calls us to move with him toward the promised land here and now. And as long as we have life and breath we are to do good